ADMINISTERING PUBLIC ASSISTANCE

Kennikat Press
National University Publications
Multidisciplinary Studies in Law and Jurisprudence

General Editor
Honorable Rudolph J. Gerber
Phoenix, Arizona

Acquisitions Editor
Victor L. Streib
Cleveland-Marshall College of Law

ADMINISTERING PUBLIC ASSISTANCE

A Constitutional and Administrative Perspective

M. Donna Price Cofer

National University Publications
KENNIKAT PRESS // 1982
Port Washington, N. Y. // London

Manufactured in the United States of America

Published by
Kennikat Press Corp.
Port Washington, N.Y. / London

Library of Congress Cataloging in Publication Data

Cofer, M. Donna Price, 1947–
    Administering public assistance.

    (Multidisciplinary studies in law and jurisprudence)
(National university publications)
    Bibliography: p.
    Includes index.
    1. Public welfare—Law and legislation—
United States. I. Title. II. Series.
KF3720.C63   344.73'03   81-18131
ISBN 0-8046-9298-X 347.3043   AACR2

To Dr. Winston M. Fisk, whose rigorous teaching
led me into administrative studies and whose patience
and profound insights kept my interests there

CONTENTS

ADMINISTERING PUBLIC ASSISTANCE

ABOUT THE AUTHOR

M. Donna Price Cofer (Ph.D., Claremont Graduate School) is on the political science faculty of Southwest Missouri State University and is a member of the Mayor's Commission on Human Rights in Springfield, Missouri.

INTRODUCTION

The administration of various benefits stemming from the United States government has become increasingly complex. This is certainly not surprising, given the great mass of people to whom benefits are offered — virtually every citizen during at least one point in his or her lifetime. The administrative complexity, however, does not lie solely in the numbers with which the government deals; it also is occasioned by several legal quandaries, the actual purposes of public assistance and the best ways administratively to meet those purposes. Should agencies adopt a posture of paternalism in distributing benefits or should they take an adversarial stance, demanding that even eligible recipients receive their benefits with shame and hesitancy?

This study will present a comprehensive analysis of those subjects affecting the administration of public assistance. Beginning with a review of congressional appropriations powers as well as legislative measures to establish beneficiary programs, the paper will identify the current membership of the United States Supreme Court as being philosophically distinct from the Court prior to 1969 and the appointment of the present chief justice, Warren Burger. The controversy of whether welfare benefits are to be considered "property" and therefore subject to the due process rights inherent in the possession of property will be seen through the reasoning of the Burger Court as will the *procedural* due process rights implied in a definition of welfare as property. The Court's interpretation of procedural due process rights affecting the receipt of disability benefits will be offered by way of contrast, since the Court has viewed the acquisition of these benefits as being less crucial to potential recipients than the receipt of welfare. Also, the constitutional interpretations of welfare home visitation have allowed the justices of the Burger Court to view society's need to be reassured that benefits are being received by truly eligible persons as more weighty than the Fourth Amendment guarantee against unreasonable searches and seizures.

Several major legal issues have come to administrators' attention through the Court's relatively recent decisions. There is obviously much room for development within administrative law regarding the procedural safeguards that an individual may claim during an agency hearing or an agency visitation to his or her home. Such questions call for an examination of agency organization and motivation, not only in dealing with agency relations with private citizens but also with those persons assigned to make the initial agency decision affecting claimants. By exploring these questions in the light of judicial decisions regarding both procedural and substantive due process, this study will provide a holistic legal view of this area of public administration as well as suggesting future targets for research efforts.

At this writing, the American people are living with much uncertainty about their economic future, the new Reagan administration having announced almost biweekly previous underestimations in fiscal 1982 federal spending and consequently placing more pressure on congressional budget committees to seek even larger budget cuts. Present recipients of welfare and disability benefits are sure to be affected. The Reagan administration has called for the following changes in Social Security programs: (1) phasing out benefits for college students; (2) limiting the amount of disability payments; (3) eliminating the lump-sum death benefit when there are no surviving beneficiaries; and (4) scrapping the $122 minimum monthly benefit program. David Stockman, director of the Office of Management and the Budget, argues that those "truly needy" recipients cut off from the minimum payments will be covered under the Supplemental Security Income program which distributes benefits to the needy aged, blind, and disabled.

The Stockman hatchet has also descended upon Aid to Families with Dependent Children (AFDC). Under the administration's proposal, beneficiaries will be required to work for their benefits in community labor projects; food stamps, federal housing subsidies, and more personal property will be counted as income in determining eligibility; and a national register of recipients will be created to avert multiple applications by one person. Most households receiving AFDC have less than an $8,410 annual income for a family of four, which is the poverty line. One in six of these families will go off the AFDC rolls under the Reagan crunch. The poor will also be hurt by major cuts in food stamps, Medicaid, unemployment insurance, public service jobs (CETA), publicly assisted housing, and child nutrition programs.

The current mania in this country to dismantle thirty years of social programs will adversely affect not only public assistance recipients but also the agencies that administer these benefits. Calls for administrative reforms requiring the addition of expert personnel are not likely to be heeded at the present time, yet equity and efficiency may demand these changes.

1

SOURCES OF PUBLIC ASSISTANCE

In 1935, the Social Security Act[1] laid the foundations for modern public-assistance administration by providing federal funds, allocated to the states, for the aged, blind, and orphaned. During an era of severe domestic economic deprivation, the federal government sought some means of relief for the most disadvantaged in the population. Some may question the current motivation for the dispersal of welfare, seeing it as a means to dampen civil disorder and, in the reverse, to reinforce majoritarian work norms by degrading those who do not participate in accepted labor. Yet the ineptitude with which welfare is generally doled out — with an error rate in eligibility determinations as high as 25 percent among the states — makes belief in any singular motivation by government policy makers, and indeed in its success, quite tenuous.

The high error rate among the states has been accompanied by discrepancies in the due process requirements between a federal- and a state-level welfare hearing. The Supreme Court has demonstrated a willingness to leave much more discretion regarding administrative processes in the hands of federal bureaucrats than in those of state administrators; the primary rationale behind consolidating all the "adult" welfare programs into the Supplemental Security Income Program (SSI) in 1972 was to take their administration out of the states' domain.

One group of researchers has concluded that a major reason for about 50 percent of case errors and a greater percentage of payment errors is client failure to report all information relevant to their need situation correctly.[2] Therefore, it is crucial to the entire welfare system that the information given clients regarding agency rules and the reporting documents that the clients complete should meet the abilities of those persons. These same researchers found in their sampling of welfare agencies among the states that only 11 percent of the documents they used were written at a level where three-quarters of their clients could comprehend them. This is important also, because since the 1973 alterations in Department of Health, Education, and Welfare regulations, caseworkers are no longer required to aid potential clients in completing either applications or requests for hearings.

The variation in the cost of administering welfare programs also reveals disparity in the quality of service offered. Social Security retirement benefits were shown in one study to require only 2 percent of total program costs for administration, whereas the food stamps program required 8 percent and Aid to Families with Dependent Children required 11 percent.[3] There was also a wide variation in administration costs among the states, with Nevada spending more than $500 and Mississippi spending $100 per case. Another example demonstrated that this disparity may be associated with the quality of service received; Oklahoma, spending $430 per AFDC case in 1976, had a case error of 11 percent whereas Ohio, spending $130 had an error rate of 22 percent.

What sort of citizens fall prey to this inconsistent administration of government largess? Of course, there are definite stereotypes which assert that such beneficiaries gladly choose this means of survival in lieu of gainful employment and return to it repeatedly. A national profile of the AFDC recipient, however, simply does not support these assumptions. This report concluded that for the average AFDC recipient, the time on welfare assistance has decreased and that there are more first-time recipients.[4] Family units with one or two children received more than half of the aid allotment, and more than 40 percent of the recipients had always lived in their present state of residence, indicating more permanency than some observers might expect. A significant number of the recipients, who seemed to be wholly dependent on their benefits, showed interest in vocational training and job placement. There were more white families receiving AFDC than black, and most AFDC recipients did not collect welfare benefits again once they had found employment. The profile certainly presents a different image of most welfare recipients than the one generally anticipated.

It also must be remembered that a large number of citizens find themselves dependent upon welfare benefits for long periods of time because of circumstances beyond their control; namely, lack of employment opportunities and trustworthy day-care centers for their children. Some researchers assert that "there are simply not enough jobs to employ everyone who is 'employable,'" and several disappointing experiences in the job market may make some persons hesitant to try again.[5] This attitude then reinforces the popular sentiment that people on welfare never want to work anyway. Thereby, welfare recipients become psychologically as well as economically dependent on the state. Interestingly, the stigma attached to the receipt of welfare benefits does not carry over into other forms of government largess, so that there has developed ". . . a law for the poor and a law for the rest of us," according to Professor Charles Reich.[6]

THE SPENDING POWER OF CONGRESS

In his classic study of congressional budgeting, Joseph Harris stated that ". . . it is the appropriations process that has been the most effective as a means of legislative control of the administrative establishment."[7] While the appropriations process may be the most effective means of congressional control over the executive branch, it is nevertheless lacking in accountability. The common complaint regarding fragmentary budgeting is a prime criticism.

In the Budget and Accounting Act of 1921, Congress attempted to establish a semblance, at least, of a national budgetary system to overcome the deficiencies of agency chiefs separately submitting their budget requests to congressional appropriations committees. The act created the Bureau of the Budget (BOB; 1970, renamed Office of Management and the Budget [OMB]) to centralize the fiscal management of the administration directly under the President. Agency chiefs were required to file their budgetary requests with the BOB which would then coordinate agency program requests and submit the product of their efforts as a whole package.

To initiate a program successfully, an agency must have the President's recommendation to Congress (through the OMB), Congress's authorization of the program, and backing from the appropriations committee in which the enacting bill originated. Article I, Section 9, of the United States Constitution reads, in part, "No money shall be drawn from the Treasury, but in consequence of appropriations made by law." This has been interpreted to mean that a separate appropriations bill must be passed by Congress after the enacting statute for a new program has been approved. Although this system offers a safeguard against Congress's being too eager to spend public monies, it also enhances the incremental, fragmented system of budgeting whereby Congress at no time considers the fiscal budget as a whole. Furthermore, the ten or more substantive subcommittees under the appropriations committees of both houses of Congress work to splinter the process additionally, for there is often little time for debate in the whole committee before an appropriations bill goes to the floor for debate.

One major reason that holistic budgetary planning may seem unfeasible is that appropriations authorizations are often designed to allow for payments over a period of several years. Consequently, a large proportion of the expenditures in a given fiscal year are based on appropriations from earlier years, and current reductions therefore have no effect upon them. Also, Congress annually votes supplementary and deficiency appropriations, which, until the passage of the 1974 Congressional Budget and Impoundment Control Act, might occur at any time during the fiscal year. With the passage of the 1974 act, time deadlines were placed upon authorization and appropriations bills, and Congress was required to adopt a budget to finance each program prior to its approval that would set figures for total appropriations and total spending as well as appropriate tax and debt levels. The act created a budget committee in both houses of Congress to oversee these responsibilities on new budget bills. With the budget stipulations enacted in 1974, Congress was discouraged from its previous practice of using continuing resolutions to continue agency appropriations when time had expired to vote new funding before the beginning of the next fiscal year.

Perhaps only 5 percent of the federal budget is subject to change by either the Congress or the President from one fiscal year to another. Consequently, the failure to assess the comparative needs of major programs at their inception is compounded by the failure to ascertain the ratio between expenditures and anticipated revenues on a holistic plane. Congress annually acts on only approximately twenty appropriations bills. The federal budget might be viewed as a mushrooming monolith that once it is put into motion finds few checks upon its continuance of agency programs. Even the General Accounting Office, through which Congress "keeps tabs" on bureaucratic spending, is incapable of curbing the spiraling effect.

Congress's complete reliance upon its committee structure for budgetary decisions not only fragments the process but also encourages political liaisons between the members of the appropriations committees and the agency clientele they are responsible for reviewing. Indeed, the appropriations budget comes out of subcommittees that are elected by the people from districts to which those monies are being allocated. Therefore, in order to assure their political survival, these representatives must develop a friendly working relationship with the very agencies that will be administering these funds to their constituents back home.

Politics, policy, and budget requests are obviously closely inter-related in intra-agency determinations. In fact, ". . . agency people seek to secure their other goals so long as this effort does not result in an over-all decrease in income."[8] Thus, all that an agency does is influenced by con-siderations about appropriations. An agency will put out "feelers" to the appropriate congressional subcommittees to get a reaction to proposed projects and will review the congressional history of expenditures in those projects' fields. Such research is especially important when the Office of Management and the Budget is recalcitrant about a proposal and has used its judgments of experience, work-load data, and cost-benefit analyses to decide that a given proposal will not enhance the public welfare. The job of agency representatives is then to prove to the subcommittee members that the proposal is valuable to their own constituents. Through such per-suasion, some subcommittee members may tend to identify more closely with the agencies they are to regulate than some observers find desirable.

Professor Aaron Wildavsky agrees with Professor Harris that political entanglements in budgetary determinations may create abuse of the public interest, but he does not advocate holistic program budgeting as a remedy; he feels that this calls for a level of planning which is beyond human pre-dictive abilities. Rather, Wildavsky supports incremental, fragmentary, bargaining budgeting, believing that the input of many factions into budget policy will balance themselves out whereas totalitarian planning will have no dissidents strong enough to change the central voice. For Wildavsky, a partial view of the public interest is preferable to a total view, because it is more feasible to be an advocate for particular interests about which one can be acquainted than to devise a grandiose scheme for the whole nation-state. Yet in a policy area such as welfare, priorities and objectives must at some point be defined. The history of welfare programs in the United States demonstrates much bargaining among different interests but it is important to remember that the poor themselves have never been organized to exert political clout on their own behalf. Conse-quently, decisions concerning the welfare of the poor have always been made by persons outside their ranks. With the advent of federally funded public assistance, at least the standards of welfare administration were taken further away from the individual citizen.

THE LEGISLATIVE HISTORY OF WELFARE

Beginning in 1933, with the Federal Emergency Relief Administration, the federal government began offering grants to the states based on a 50-50 matching ratio in order to relieve some of the economic deprivation of the Great Depression. Other programs, such as the Emergency Work Relief Program (1934) and the Works Progress Administration (1935), followed leading up to the Social Security Act of 1935. This single piece of legislation replaced a tradition in the United States of the individual states administering their own relief programs.[9] With an economic depression on the scale of that of the 1930s, the former welfare structure was simply no longer appropriate.

The Social Security Act encompassed several programs. First of all, it provided social insurance in the form of federal old-age insurance and a federal-state system of unemployment compensation. Second, it established public categorical assistance composed of federal grants-in-aid including Old-Age Assistance, Aid to the Needy Blind, and Aid to Dependent Children. Third, it created health and welfare services under the titles of Maternal and Child Health Services, Services for Crippled Children, Child Welfare Services, Vocational Rehabilitation, and Public Health Services. In 1953, the last two programs fell under the auspices of two different branches in the Department of Health, Education and Welfare when HEW was divided into the Social Security Administration, the Public Health Services, the Office of Education, and the Office of Vocational Rehabilitation. Through these offices, the Social Security Administration provides economic security for the eligible individual in the form of (1) public assistance, financed by taxation; (2) social insurance, financed by contributions of the beneficiary and of his or her employer; and (3) pension systems based on such statutes as Railroad Workers' Insurance.

The Social Security Act has undergone several major alterations since its inception. In 1950, Aid to the Permanently and Totally Disabled was added to the public categorical assistance list of programs. In 1965, the act was amended to improve the provisions of Old-Age, Survivors, and Disability Insurance as well as those of public assistance, and the Maternal,

Child Health, and Child Welfare Services were also expanded. Two coordinated health insurance programs for the aged were added to the act, including Medicare — hospitalization insurance — and Medicaid, which covers physicians' charges.[10] Perhaps one of the most far-reaching amendments to the Social Security Act occurred in 1972, in which assistance to the needy aged, blind, and disabled came under the auspices of the Social Security Administration in terms of total funding and implementation in the form of Supplemental Security Income.[11] It is important to note that Aid to Families with Dependent Children (AFDC) was *not* taken from state and local administration, in which each state determines its own standard of need for eligibility — nor was Medicaid. This 1972 amendment was motivated by a desire to standardize assistance payments to the aged, blind, and disabled, as well as to seek a reduction in the error rate of eligibility determinations as evidenced among the states.

As a result of the 1972 amendment, AFDC has principally become identified with "welfare" or public assistance, and public dissatisfaction with the program continues. Part of the discontent may exist simply because it is popularly considered acceptable to receive some forms of public assistance but not others. The receipt of Supplemental Security Income probably indicates that one is a victim of circumstances — old age, blindness, or disability — beyond one's control, and therefore the receipt of benefits is justifiable. To receive AFDC benefits, however, seems to connote to many citizens the desire of able-bodied persons to escape from gainful employment and personal and social responsibility. That both these programs fall under the title of public assistance does not seem to influence public prejudice. AFDC recipients are viewed critically for moving to states that offer higher benefits, even though these same critics might well at some date find themselves to be the victims of economic fluctuations beyond their control. The Revenue Sharing Act of 1972 (PL92-512), however, in limiting federal funds for social services under state administration to $2.5 billion (except for the Work Incentive Program), indicates the public belief that work is available if one is willing to seek it. This attitude of the 1970s will definitely affect how the courts interpret a person's right to possess public assistance and the procedural requirements necessary to assure that right.

If a person is in financial need and is not eligible for any of the social-insurance or public-assistance programs under the Social Security Act, he or she may seek general assistance through the state in which he or she is a resident. Such relief is wholly state- and locally financed and varies greatly from one state to another. Just as the amount of monetary benefits and services offered varies greatly, so does the level of procedural due process protections for those individuals denied benefits. There has been a call by the United States Supreme Court for a federally imposed Fourteenth Amendment due process requirement that the several states meet the procedural strictures of *Goldberg* v. *Kelly* (1970) in any denial of general assistance benefits. The federal court of the eastern district of Wisconsin has ruled in *Alexander* v. *Silverman* that a post-denial hearing should be available to applicants for general assistance who have not been denied on prima facie ineligibility. The court distinguished this case from *Goldberg* because of its involvement with general assistance as opposed to categorical assistance and, thereby, held for a *post*denial hearing as opposed to a pretermination hearing. Nevertheless, this decision may serve as an example to other states to offer minimal protections against their own welfare administrators' possible abuse of discretion in eligibility cases that are not clearly defined by agency policy.

The turbulent decade of the 1960s saw the creation of several major federally funded programs to bring the poor into the American political process. The Economic Opportunity Act of 1964[12] offered direct federal funding to local community-action programs designed to involve the poor in political decision making. Community action may be defined as "a technique for mobilizing the resources of the whole community to respond to families and individuals as 'full human beings.'"[13] There also was an attempt to supplement welfare payments with practical job training. Offspring of the Office of Economic Opportunity included Project Head Start, the Job Corps, the Neighborhood Youth Corps, and VISTA. In 1966, the act was altered to require one-third of the members of local community boards on poverty to be spokesmen for the poor of the area. This stipulation obviously demanded a much higher level of political organization by the poor than any known previously. While these programs have been assimilated into established agencies since the 1960s, the administrative abuses that accompanied them on the local level still remain in the sense that an abundance of public monies has been spent, and yet the environment of the poor has not been substantially altered.

Providing legal assistance for the poor was also a major objective of the 1960s. The Legal Services Program (LSP) was initially a part of the Office of Economic Opportunity (OEO). The program established diverse legal-aid facilities throughout the country, designed to meet local needs. In seeking to meet local challenges, however, the LSP became a threat to local interests in business and government and thus fell prey to political coercion. Despite such pressures, the LSP had to its credit the landmark United States Supreme Court decisions of *Shapiro* v. *Thompson,* invalidating state residency requirements as a test for the receipt of welfare; *King* v. *Smith,* striking down denial of AFDC benefits to children whose mother is living with an employable man; and *Goldberg* v. *Kelly,* establishing procedural guidelines for pretermination, evidentiary AFDC hearings. The monetary relief to the poor as a result of *Shapiro* by itself exceeded the entire cost to the public of the LSP alone!

Political pressures, controversy over LSP attorneys creating business for themselves by educating the poor about illegal actions likely to victimize them, and concern over "test" cases led to the Nixon administration's push for the creation of a Legal Services Corporation. This nonprofit corporation, which became a reality in 1974, is divorced from the executive branch and is headed, as a nonpartisan, independent corporation, by a professional legal-services staff. The eleven-member board, appointed by the President, distributes federal monies to 287 local poverty-law-related programs throughout the nation. Even this major organizational adjustment, however, has left unanswered many of the problems about legal representation for the poor. The corporation is plagued with inadequate financing, rapid personnel turnover, and lack of guidance from Washington.

Despite the somewhat discouraging situation of the Legal Services Corporation, the Supreme Court in *Fitzpatrick* v. *Bitzer* has recently opened the avenue for the award of legal fees to litigants exercising their Fourteenth Amendment rights against states and state officials. Previously, in *Edelman* v. *Jordan,* the Court majority had denied an Illinois citizen's suit against that state for allegedly administering its aid to the aged, blind, or disabled program inconsistently with federal regulations and the Fourteenth Amendment. The majority argued that the Eleventh Amendment prohibits a state's own citizens from bringing suit for money against it in federal court. The state of Illinois, therefore, could not be forced to pay the respondent disability benefits retroactively due out of the state treasury, although injunctive relief could be sought against state officials to comply with the Social Security Act. Justice Brennan, among a group of four dissenters, asserted that Illinois had placed itself outside Eleventh Amendment protection by participating in the public-assistance program.

In more recent cases, the Court has upheld the Civil Rights Attorney's Fee Awards Act of 1976,[14] ruling that congressional power to uphold the Fourteenth Amendment overrides the Eleventh Amendment claim. This decision contains broad implications for the rights of public-assistance recipients in terms of their demanding constitutional protections against state welfare administrative abuses, even if the federal courts are not willing to define the exact procedures for other than AFDC hearings.

Some may see a conspiracy of sorts in American welfare administration to keep the losers in our competitive economy under control. Reviewing the regulations implemented by the Department of Health, Education and Welfare in 1973, regarding AFDC and Medicaid, one may at least sense an agency indifference toward welfare applicants' abilities to complete complex forms without assistance, to the eligibility verification methods used by the states, and to access to the hearing process. The instituting of local evidentiary hearings whose decisions are applicable to a state agency[15] is reflective of one critic's observation of the vestiges of English poor law in this country whereby relief was available only through local public officials, so that the requirements of the local labor market could be determining in one's receipt of assistance − a position of significant political control.[16] The current Supreme Court's support of returning welfare administration to local control is, however, probably far more indicative of that Court majority's own biases about federal relations than a desire to see welfare claimants abused in seeking the benefits to which they are eligible. Yet is it an accurate depiction to describe the United States Supreme Court as a "different Court" from the years of Chief Justice Earl Warren's service? Is not the Supreme Court a continuing entity, serving to stabilize the interpretation and enforcement of public law in these United States?

IS THERE A BURGER COURT?

Through the unusual occurrence of a single President having the opportunity to appoint four justices to the United States Supreme Court, including the chief justice, the philosophical orientation of the Court became subject to drastic change. This transformation, which did indeed take place, began in 1969 with President Richard Nixon's appointment of Warren Burger as chief justice. Nixon had promised to rebalance the Court toward "strict constructionism," meaning toward interpretation of what the Constitution itself provides rather than finding new areas of constitutional coverage. The Court, however, from 1969 to the present has marked itself as an activist Court, but activist in a judicial philosophy very different from that of its predecessor. Relatively early in its term, the Burger Court shocked some observers by refusing to halt the publication of the Pentagon Papers (*New York Times Co.* v. *United States, United States* v. *The Washington Post*), by striking down the death penalty (*Furman* v. *Georgia, Jackson* v. *Georgia, Branch* v. *Texas*), by upholding busing to desegregate schools (*Swann* v. *Charlotte-Mecklenburg County Board of Education*), and by giving women the right to an abortion (*Roe* v. *Wade, Doe* v. *Bolton*). Yet especially in the areas of criminal procedure and freedom of the press, the Burger Court has identified itself as a new wave of judicial thinking. In other words, the Burger Court, while not directly overruling Warren Court precedents in these two areas, has distinguished itself from its predecessor by demonstrating less empathy for the criminal defendant and the media's right to inform, and more for the public interest as this Court perceives it.

In June 1969, Warren Earl Burger was confirmed by the United States Senate to succeed Earl Warren as chief justice of the United States Supreme Court. Prior to his appointment, he had served in the U.S. Court of Appeals for the District of Columbia where he gained the reputation of being a conservative, especially in criminal justice cases. His appointment to the Court was followed a year later by that of Harry A. Blackmun, a lifelong friend of Burger; their voting patterns were so closely aligned early in this Court's existence that he and Burger were labeled the "Minnesota Twins." Blackman replaced Abe Fortas who resigned.

With the resignation of two prestigious justices — Hugo Black and John Harlan — in the fall of 1971, President Nixon had the opportunity to make two more appointments to the Supreme Court. He first named Lewis F. Powell, Jr., former president of the American Bar Association and senior partner in an old Virginia law firm, who is noted for a moderate stance in civil liberties cases. Nixon's final appointment was William H. Rehnquist, a former assistant U.S. attorney general, considered to be the most conservative member of the Court. In 1975, John Paul Stevens was appointed to the Court by President Gerald Ford after the resignation of the longest-serving Supreme Court justice, William O. Douglas. Stevens is noted for being an expert in antitrust law and essentially a moderate. With the Stevens appointment, five relatively new justices joined Potter Stewart and Byron White, who seem to object to having a voting pattern, and William Brennan, Jr., and Thurgood Marshall, the two consistently liberal judges remaining on the Court.

Especially in the area of criminal proceedings, the Burger Court has restricted some earlier Warren Court precedents by ". . . confining their effect to circumstances similar to those in the original case, or condoning certain violations of rights as harmless error in light of other facts in a particular case."[17] The chief justice alone took a favorable position toward the government in criminal-procedure cases 70 percent of the time in his first term and 81.6 percent in his second term, whereas Earl Warren voted for the government in criminal-procedure cases only 19 percent of the time during a period of more than sixteen years.[18] A 6-3 division of the Court has become the rule in criminal justice cases. The four Nixon appointees have replaced the Warren-Brennan-Black-Douglas quartet with Justices White and/or Stewart clearly helping those four to control the Court. At the same time, Justices Brennan and Marshall find themselves in dissent. It is now the responsibility of the Burger Court to define the administrative implications of the Warren Court rulings in civil liberties cases. Therein, concepts of the separation of powers, judicial review, and federalism become crucial.

In 1967, the then future chief justice, Burger, made the following statement regarding the rights of criminal defendants:

Governments exist chiefly to foster the rights and interests of their citizens − to protect their homes and property, their persons and their lives. If a government fails in this basic duty, it is not redeemed by providing even the most perfect system for the protection of the rights of defendants in the criminal courts.[19]

In wishing to give the states more discretion in their administration of criminal justice, the Burger Court has been lenient in judging the several states' interpretations of Warren Court precedents. The Court has also paid great deference to the expertise of law-enforcement officials, contending that police officers can often best judge "the totality of circumstances" in determining probable cause for arrest. In 1973, the Court ruled that police officers are under no constitutional obligation to inform a private citizen of his or her right to refuse a warrantless search of his or her home. Rather, the police must consider "the totality of the circumstances" in determining in a particular case whether consent has been voluntarily given to such a visit. In contrast to the 1966 *Miranda* ruling, the responsibility for the defendant's knowledge of his or her rights no longer rests with the police but with the defendant.

Probably the case best indicating the present Court's disdain for *Miranda* was *Harris* v. *New York,* decided in 1971. The Court majority, speaking through Chief Justice Burger, ruled that voluntary statements made by a defendant can be used to impeach his or her credibility if he or she has contradicted them previously. Thus Harris, although not given the *Miranda* warnings, could be confronted with contradictory statements made at the time of his arrest and while testifying at his trial. The Court ruled that it could not justify the use of *Miranda* as a shield to cover perjurious statements made in the courtroom. Again, the weight of protecting the rights of the defendant falls solely upon the defendant, even if he or she is ignorant of their existence. In cases where the private citizen is verbally "given his rights" by the police, the Court ruled in *North Carolina* v. *Butler* that the police may make the decision as to when the citizen has waived his *Miranda* right to silence, if not done so explicitly. The police must make the judgment whether this right has been waived, given the context in which the assumption is made.

The Burger Court has also distinguished itself from its predecessor in its restrictive stance toward the news media. In 1972, in *United States* v. *Caldwell,* the Court majority held that newsmen risk being held in contempt of court if they refuse to provide information to a grand jury concerning a crime or reveal their sources of evidence concerning a crime. In the balance, the Court did not view the newsman's claim to offer anonymity to his sources to be weightier than the public's right to inform itself through grand jury investigations. In the spring of 1979, in *Herbert* v. *Lando,* the Court released its most stringent decision to date concerning the press. The Court majority ruled that the First Amendment does not protect the editorial process – meaning the prepublication thoughts, conclusions, and conversations of editors and reporters – from judicial scrutiny for those who charge that they have been libeled by the product of that process. In order to test the "actual malice" standard in *New York Times* v. *Sullivan,* the Court held that the state of mind – i.e., the motivations – of the defendant may be the subject of inquiry. As a result of this decision, the newsman can no longer guarantee a potential source confidentiality, for the reporter's own thoughts are open to scrutiny. In contrast, the Warren Court showed little interest in attempting to assess the psychological motivations of a defendant in lieu of examining the consequences of his actions, as in *Griggs* v. *Duke Power Company* (1971).

Certainly since the Nixon appointments to the Court were completed in the fall of 1971, the Court has shifted its attidude especially in cases of criminal justice and freedom of the press. In the early years of their tenure on the highest bench, the Nixon appointees voted together more often than not. In the 1972 term, they voted together in fifty-three of the seventy cases in which all nine justices participated and were joined in one decision in forty-five of those fifty-three decisions.[20] In the 1974 term, at least three of the four Nixon appointees voted together in all but ten cases; nearly two-thirds of the rulings in that term were split votes with many major rulings based on 5-4 splits.[21] While there is some evidence that the "Nixon bloc" has lost some of its original cohesiveness,[22] it has nevertheless established a distinct identity for itself apart from its predecessor. While matching the activism of the Warren Court, it has used its critical skills most often to promote the interests of government and society over those of the individual. It is a Court that fears the consequences which extreme individual expression may bring or perhaps even the expression of those underprivileged citizens seeking society's aid.

2

AN ENTITLEMENT TO WELFARE?

The question of whether government benefits are to be defined as a constitutionally protected property holding of the recipient or viewed as a privilege to be granted or denied at government whim is basic to any discussion of due process requirements in welfare proceedings. The legal status judicially afforded welfare benefits will determine the degree of constitutional protection they receive. This protection comes from two potential sources: due process of the Fifth and Fourteenth Amendments and equal protection of the laws in the Fourteenth. The development of judicial interpretation on this topic has become involved and complex, perhaps to its actual abandonment. This chapter will review this evolutionary process in order to establish a theoretical foundation for later administrative observations.

WELFARE AS PROPERTY

The first significant scholarly exploration of what some call the "right-privilege distinction" was "The New Property" by Professor Charles A. Reich.[1] Therein, Reich asserted that government largess had become such an integral part of every American citizen's life that the whole population was dependent upon it for essential welfare as their *legitimate* possession. In fact, Reich was refuting the established *Carolene Products* doctrine of Justice Stone by no longer accepting a lesser level of protection for economic property rights as opposed to First Amendment civil liberties.

Actually, Reich was satisfied in 1964 with labeling government largess "wealth," but not with claiming that it necessarily takes the form of property. There may be no individual right involved in the receipt of largess, only the dispersement of a gratuity over which government has absolute discretion with the exception of violations of Fourteenth Amendment equal protection.

Through a long list of decisions, the Supreme Court has wrestled with or, in some cases, attempted to evade the "right-privilege distinction." In earlier years, the Warren Court established a formula of "suspect classifications," such as race, sex, religious preference, and national origin and ancestry balanced against a *compelling* state interest to make such classifications factors in special treatment for some citizens. The use of "suspect classifications" automatically led to the demise of much legislation during this period in Court history, for few states could demonstrate their interest to be compelling rather than merely rational. There were also personal rights, although only constitutionally implied, that the Court was willing to recognize. These included interstate travel, voting on an equal basis with others, procreation, and privacy.[2] These rights have maintained their status, but attempts to enhance the category with welfare benefits and public education have failed, as will be discussed later.

The Social Security Act of 1935 provided that all persons establishing eligibility under its dictates are entitled to its benefits, and yet the Court has consistently failed to see that the individual's interest reaches beyond his or her singular set of circumstances. In other words, recipients of welfare have not been perceived as a legal class. It is therefore extremely difficult for the individual recipient to win in a balance against community interest. He or she is, in effect, without legal status to bolster his or her claim to entitlement. Indeed, the public interest may find much justification for imposing standards of morality, violating the privacy of a recipient's home, and denying procedural due process rights through the agencies upon which the poor rely. Public interest in such considerations as administrative frugality may lead to a total disregard for individual liberties based on property rights. Equal protection of the laws and procedural due process provide constitutional limits to intimidating public-interest claims as well as issues surrounding the relevance of bureaucratic restrictions, the scope of agency discretion, and private organizations' use of massive subsidization. But these considerations are far from a claim to benefits as a property right.

Charles Reich asserted that governmental largess, which is closely associated with one's personal status, must *eventually* be recognized as property, for as in welfare administration, "[o]nly by making such benefits into rights can the welfare state achieve its goal of providing a secure minimum basis for individual well-being and dignity in a society where each man cannot be wholly the master of his own destiny."[3] Interestingly, Reich justified the receipt of welfare with an assumption that no member of a competitive society is completely in charge of his or her economic fate and therefore cannot be held culpable for arriving at a state of want. Indeed, the competitive economic system in which the Western world finds itself assumes that some will succeed and others will fail, but Reich charged that it is not to society's benefit to have some citizens in abject need. American society rarely acknowledges that welfare benefits are the means by which the recipient may be enabled to compete more successfully for independent employment. In this, the use of largess is well within the public interest.

Reich defined entitlement to mean ". . . objective eligibility safeguards against revocation or loss of benefits, and it means that the individual's rights, whatever they may be, should be known to him and enforceable through law."[4] This definition is most helpful in suggesting the need for expressed individual rights, legally enforced. This, of course, has been the task of the federal judiciary as it has observed administrative tribunals functioning as part of the distributing agencies themselves. Depending upon the agency, a claimant may discover that there may be no cross-examination of adverse witnesses or no hearing in any form held because of the denial of benefits. Evidence may also be accepted for consideration that no court would admit, and no legal counsel may be present or allowed to represent the individual claimant. The standards of administrative law in regard to hearings are obviously different from – though not necessarily less than – those of a trial court. How these standards are created has become of increasing importance to the individual citizen as administrative agencies have become more ingrained in the American fabric. A later chapter will examine the issues of law raised by this development. The present task is a survey of Supreme Court decisions dealing with the legal status of those individuals claiming eligibility to welfare benefits.

JUDICIAL DEFINITION OF ELIGIBILITY

Flemming v. *Nestor* was the first decision in which the United States Supreme Court dealt with an alleged right to the receipt of government largess. In this 1960 case, the Court disallowed Nestor's receipt of old-age benefits from the Social Security fund to which he had contributed during his employable years. The Court reasoned that Nestor must meet the federal government's condition — namely, not having Communist party affiliations — before he could claim benefits. Refusing to accept Nestor's claim that the benefits constituted an "accrued property right," the Court supported the government's action as long as it could not be adjudged as arbitrary. If Nestor's property claim had been successful, the public interest would have been much less persuasive since, according to Professor Reich, property rights build the fences between individualism and majority rule. In other words, the public interest would be more wisely identified with individualism than with majority rule, as has been the American tradition. While Reich saw property as a societal construction rather than a natural right, he believed the concept to be essential to any system of political rights based on individual self-interest. The relationship between political rights and government largess is graphically demonstrated in *Flemming* v. *Nestor.*

Three years later, the Court was surprisingly receptive to an individual's claim to largess. In *Sherbert* v. *Verner,* seven justices held that a "compelling state interest" would have to be demonstrated before Ms. Sherbert could be denied unemployment benefits, even though her employment had been terminated because of her deliberate refusal to work on Saturdays. The appellant, being a Seventh Day Adventist, would have violated a basic tenet of her religious dogma if she had worked on the Jewish Sabbath. The Court held that "governmental imposition of such a choice puts the same kind of a burden upon the free exercise of religion as would a fine imposed against appellant for her Saturday worship." In other words, a potential recipient of largess cannot be forced to sacrifice a fundamental right in order to receive the governmental benefit for which he or she is eligible. This same principle had already been expressed in *Shelton* v. *Tucker* in which an Arkansas law requiring disclosure by public school teachers of all organizations in which they held membership was declared unconstitutional. The Court did not view public employment as being constitutionally protected but did hold that the disclosure requirement offended the teachers' First Amendment implied freedom of association. That right could not be denied as an indirect effect upon their employment. The Court, in *Sherbert,* would not hear the argument that unemployment payments are a privilege rather than a right. It somewhat ironically referred back to *Flemming* v. *Nestor* in which it said, "The interest of a covered employee under the Act is of sufficient substance to fall within the protection from arbitrary governmental action afforded by the Due Process Clause." Also citing *Everson* v. *Board of Education,* the Court reaffirmed that no state can exclude a member of any faith ". . . *because of their faith, or lack of it,* from receiving the benefits of public welfare legislation."

Possibly the Supreme Court's most explicit statement on the "entitlement" issue came in the landmark case of *Goldberg* v. *Kelly.* Mr. Kelly, an AFDC (Aid to Families with Dependent Children) recipient, had had his benefits terminated without a prior evidentiary hearing. He and several other recipients similarly treated were informed by New York public-assistance officials that under state regulations they could request a hearing to have their payments restored. Instead, the group appealed to the federal courts, and for the first time, welfare benefits were termed by the Supreme Court to be "a matter of statutory entitlement for persons qualified to receive them." Thus, the "right-privilege distinction" was virtually eliminated with eligibility assuring the receipt of benefits. Associate Justice Brennan, writing the opinion for a majority of five, asserted that it was realistic to view welfare as "property" since various symbols of entitlement to government benefits exist throughout our society in the form of professional licenses, government subsidies, long-term government contracts, and many more. Constitutional challenges to the administration of welfare cannot be dismissed by calling benefits a privilege rather than a right. If eligibility entitles one to largess, then procedural due process must determine administrative action taken in regard to receipt of benefits. The extent to which due process is required has to do with the degree of the loss to the recipient.

In dissent, Associate Justice Hugo Black emphatically rejected the Court's terming government charity as property. He asserted that the Fourteenth Amendment was primarily written to protect the ex-slaves. It was indeed incredible to see such a statement in 1970, after the long development of procedural due process and equal protection of the laws. Was Black calling for a strict "legislative-intent" approach to judicial interpretation? It was difficult to believe that a primary member of the activist front during the years of the Warren Court could be making such an assertion. And yet his statement that the Court was pressing its own philosophy of procedural due process upon the nation causes one to wonder at his late-found judicial restraint, even considering his reputation for a literal interpretation of the supreme law.

In its next term, in *Bell* v. *Burson,* the Court held that a driver's license, once issued, was an entitlement, whether denominated a "right" or "privilege," which may be necessary to a citizen's continued livelihood. Therefore, the state of Georgia had been in violation of procedural due process by suspending the appellant's driver's license when as an uninsured driver he was involved in a traffic accident and failed to post security to cover damages claimed by the aggrieved party. In his opinion, Justice Brennan developed a doctrine that would provide the Court with latitude for future decisions: "A procedural rule that may satisfy due process in one context may not necessarily satisfy procedural due process in every case." Different types of entitlement call for diverse procedural requirements. In a later decision, *Mathews* v. *Eldridge,* Associate Justice Rehnquist would use this principle in a more negative vein to uphold lesser procedural standards for disability hearings than those concerning Aid to Families with Dependent Children.

The "right-privilege distinction" was again abandoned in *Board of Regents of State Colleges* v. *Roth,* decided in June 1972. The seven-member majority ruled that Roth had no property interest in reemployment as an assistant professor since his contract had been negotiated for one year only. Associate Justice Stewart, for the Court, held that the "Fourteenth Amendment's procedural protection of property is a safeguard of security of interests that a person has already acquired in specific benefits." The specificity of the benefits is central to an alleged property interest in them. A person must have a legitimate claim of entitlement, not merely an abstract need or desire for the benefits. But once this position is assured, the person then has a right to a hearing to ensure that the property is not being arbitrarily removed. While property interests are not created by the Constitution, continued Stewart, they are created and defined by societal rules which engender real expectations of benefit from the property holder.

The Court thus asserted that there is no need to define entitlement in terms of "right" or "privilege." An entitlement to certain benefits either exists or else it doesn't, given eligibility or lack thereof of the potential recipient. The *Roth* decision helped to clarify a much-debated issue by essentially dismissing it wholesale. Instead of being concerned with whether a recipient was receiving a gift from the public dole or had a constitutionally protected right to the benefits, the Court avoided the troublesome issue by assessing entitlement on the basis of eligibility to said benefits. Once established, eligibility should guarantee that benefits will not be arbitrarily or capriciously denied, that procedural due process requirements will be met even though the specific requirements will be conditioned by the type of benefits sought. The burden placed upon the individual facing possible loss of benefits will determine due process stipulations, as the Court had mapped out clearly in *Goldberg*.

EQUAL PROTECTION OF THE LAWS FOR THE POOR

A second significant development of constitutional interpretation has occurred within the framework of social-welfare legislation. This, of course, is the question of providing equal protection of the laws to the poor. As discussed above, there has been much argument in the Court as to whether the poor can be defined as a class and therefore perceived as the victims of discrimination under legal definition. In fact, because of its failure to view the poor as a legally defined class, the Court has frequently found a means to allow for program experimentation among the states, ignoring possible discriminatory effects upon poor people as a class.

In 1969, the Court, still headed by Earl Warren, heard arguments in *Shapiro* v. *Thompson* concerning a Connecticut statute that required a person to live in the state for at least one year before applying for public welfare. Associate Justice Brennan, writing for a majority of six, ruled that this law created two classes of needy individuals: those already resident in the state for at least one year who could receive benefits, and those who — although perhaps as needy — could not receive them. Justice Brennan saw this as state-imposed discrimination in violation of Fourteenth Amendment equal protection of the laws. The Court did not address the question of whether the poor formed a legally recognizable class; it only saw some poor receiving assistance and others being totally deprived of it. One of those implied rights within the Bill of Rights was also at issue here. Brennan acknowledged freedom to travel among the states of the United States as an accepted right that would be artificially hindered or discouraged by such a law as the one questioned in this case. Consequently, the statute fell. As in *Sherbert*, the exercise of one right cannot exclude a person from the exercise of other rights.

After some changes in personnel, the Court made a very different kind of decision in April 1970. Indeed, *Dandridge* v. *Williams* is even surprising when one notes that the decision was made within two weeks of *Goldberg* v. *Kelly*. A regulation of the Maryland Department of Public Welfare had placed an absolute limit of $250 per month upon the amount given in any AFDC grant regardless of family size or actual need. The Court majority saw no violation of Fourteenth Amendment equal protection of the laws "so long as some aid is provided to all eligible families and all eligible children. . . ." Associate Justice Stewart, for the majority, saw nothing unconstitutional about the admittedly imperfect classification by the state as long as the basis for it was reasonable. In fact, he asserted that he would be especially tolerant of such categorization in state attempts to finance and administer social welfare in particular. He reasoned that the state has a highly justifiable interest in encouraging citizens to seek employment, so that it will not find itself in the position of discriminating in favor of the unemployed against the working poor.

Attempts to reconcile this decision to *Goldberg* are frustrated by such questions as why New York's AFDC payments can be classified as "property" and yet Maryland's assistance offers no entitlement to subsistence beyond the maximum allowed. That the state can limit assistance without regard to actual family needs certainly places a strain upon real protection of the property interests of the individual. Obviously, entitlement is a reality only within the strict boundaries set by the state. While the *Goldberg* decision rests on due process claims, the fundamental property interest supported by Justice Brennan's decision is basic to all welfare claims. Yet in *Dandridge,* it seems to recede. As one commentator succinctly stated, "In a logically consistent world, I venture to say that the *Goldberg* and *Dandridge* decisions could not coexist."[5]

Diversity among state AFDC programs was again upheld in 1972 in *Jefferson* v. *Hackney.* Texas had readjusted its categorical grants-in-aid so that AFDC assistance was reduced 25 percent, five times more than other categories. AFDC recipients brought suit alleging that since 87 percent of those on AFDC were black or Mexican, these identifiable groups were being discriminated against in violation of equal protection of the laws. Somewhat characteristically of the Supreme Court since 1971, Associate Justice Rehnquist asserted that because there had been no *intent* on the part of the state to discriminate, no discrimination could be held to have occurred. Justice Rehnquist saw nothing in opposition to federal standards in the state's policy and emphasized that it has never been the ambition of the Social Security Administration to standardize the states' computational methods for AFDC claims or any other public-assistance program. The Burger Court's emphasis on leaving more room for discretion among state administrators is here once again evident. It is perhaps a bit frightening to some Court observers that the justices are willing to attempt to assess an administrator's motivation as opposed to the actual consequences of his or her actions. This is a far cry from the days of *Griggs* when disparate effect in employment practices, whether intentional or not, was enough to abolish them. Understanding another human being's motivations is a much more tricky business than perhaps Justice Rehnquist would wish to admit.

The New York State Department of Social Services (v. *Dublino*) came under attack again after *Goldberg,* but with a different outcome. In 1973, the Court heard arguments against the work rules of this department with claims that they were preempted by the Federal Work Incentive Program of the Social Security Act. A majority of seven asserted that nothing in the act prohibited the state from putting such a stipulation on the receipt of public assistance, even though persons eligible under federal law might be exempted. The Court smiled upon the state's attempt to get those capable of working employed, so that limited welfare funds could go to individuals who did not have the option of employment. Congress had not made it clear in the federal program that it wished to preempt the already-existing state work-incentive programs nor those developed at a later date. The individual states should be allowed to experiment; they best know their own situations. Apparently for the Burger Court, categorical grants-in-aid programs are much more guidelines for state action than programs to be administered holistically. The rub that persons federally eligible to receive benefits in New York and certainly eligible under other states' programs would be excluded through this program was not answered by the majority but was "assertively" discussed by Justices Marshall and Brennan in dissent. They perceived the state's work rules to violate the Supremacy Clause as well as Fourteenth Amendment's equal protection of the laws.

The most recent example of the Court's supporting a peculiar state regulation in welfare administration again comes from New York in *Lavine* v. *Milne.* Although argued on due process grounds, the case has implications for equal protection by classifying persons as to the voluntary or involuntary nature of the end of their employment, thus creating two categories of those applying for benefits. The assessment of an individual's motivations again come into play as the Court upheld a state law providing that those persons who voluntarily terminated their employment were ineligible to receive welfare benefits for seventy-five days. The U.S. District Court of the Southern District of New York had struck down the law on the basis that it created a "rebuttable presumption" that all welfare applicants who voluntarily terminate their employment do so in order to collect welfare. The Supreme Court did not agree, although a previous decision would cause some bafflement to Court observers seeking consistency on this issue. In *United States Department of Agriculture* v. *Murry,* the Court overturned a congressional amendment to the Food Stamp Act because it formulated a "rebuttable presumption." The amendment provided that any household which included a person of over eighteen years of age who was claimed as a dependent for income-tax purposes by an ineligible taxpayer would not, as a group, be eligible for food stamps. The Court saw Congress presuming that a household containing such a dependent was not needy. In the present case, however, the Court did not perceive that New York had made such an unfounded presumption, perhaps because the *federal government* was administering the food-stamp regulation and a *state* was experimenting with its own environment in *Lavine.*

A unanimous Court — with Justice Stevens not participating — held in *Lavine* that the only "rebuttable presumption" it understood was that each applicant would bear the weight of proving his own eligibility for assistance.[6] Nothing in the Constitution requires benefits to be given before eligibility is established; thus applicants may be required to wait seventy-five to ninety days for a decision on eligibility without demanding a hearing. Even if under this regulation a large number of people are temporarily unjustly denied their benefits, the ". . . Fourteenth Amendment does not guarantee that all decisions by state officials will be correct and New York would seem to have no incentive to deny benefits wrongfully." Once again, the Court has concerned itself with the motivations of the state administrators. As long as these appear to be justifiable, their consequences are insignificant. The regulation does provide for retroactive payment of benefits if wrongfully denied, so the state would have no incentive to deny benefits unjustly. The state should be free to use its judgment even if a hardship will be worked upon some citizens in order to apprehend less responsible ones, according to Associate Justice White.

Probably the most cogent example of the amount of latitude the Court is willing to give the states in administering public welfare can be seen in the contrast between *United States Department of Agriculture* v. *Moreno* (1973) and *Village of Belle Terre* v. *Boraas* (1974). The *Moreno* decision disallowed an amendment to the federal Food Stamp Act that denied food stamps to any household containing a person not related to another member of the household. The majority did not agree with Congress that unrelated persons living in the same household were more likely to defraud the government. However, in *Boraas,* the Court upheld a local ordinance that excluded households of three or more unrelated persons. On a much less rigorous rational-basis test, the Court saw the local authorities rightly using their legislative discretion to promote the peace and quiet of village neighborhoods. Yet the Court did not test the assumptions being made in the local ordinance against real circumstances as it did in *Moreno* where it found Congress's assumptions unfounded. The Court has obviously been willing to defer to the judgment of agents of the several states rather than to Congress in determining questions of living arrangements, even if the regulation is at the point of eliminating certain kinds of households altogether. The brand of federal relations in these United States has certainly changed since the days of a Court willing to tackle the desegregation of public schools and the reapportionment of state legislatures.

The fate of identifying the poor as a legally recognizable class was set in *San Antonio Independent School District* v. *Rodriguez.* The 5–4 vote supported an opinion whereby the right to an education was declared not to be constitutionally guaranteed, and wealth was said not to be a suspect way of classifying people. At question was the common means of financing public education through property taxes, with richer districts being in a position to offer more educational advantages to their students than poorer districts. Associate Justice Powell, for the majority, could find no definable class of poor people and therefore could not say that any legally coverable class was not receiving adequate protection under the Fourteenth Amendment. Justice Powell stated that "it is not the province of this Court to create substantive constitutional rights in the name of guaranteeing equal protection of the laws." Neither can it be said that in this case anyone has absolutely been denied an education. It is for local authorities who better understand local problems and the intricacies of raising and allocating public revenues to decide upon the formula most appropriate to their needs.

A strong dissent was registered by Associate Justice Thurgood Marshall. He viewed the Fourteenth Amendment far differently than the majority as he asserted that "the Equal Protection Clause is not addressed to the minimal sufficiency but rather to the unjustifiable inequalities of state action." How much education is sufficient? Should the Court be so concerned with identifying a particular group of oppressed persons ". . . [so] long as the basis of the discrimination is clearly identified. . . ."? Marshall noted that the Court in *Bulloch* v. *Carter* struck down a filing fee for primary elections in the state of Texas as positing a violation of equal protection of the laws even though members of the disadvantaged class were not readily definable. According to Marshall, "[T]he nature of the classification in *Bulloch* was clear, although the precise membership of the disadvantaged class was not." The right to procreate, to vote in the state elections, and to appeal a criminal conviction are all judicially recognized but not explicitly guaranteed in the United States Constitution. Why would the Court be willing to give these rights preeminence over education? Why has the Court also been willing to acknowledge rights to interstate travel, association, and privacy? Is education not as fundamental to life in a liberal democracy as these?

Marshall also pointed to the glaring inconsistency between the instant case and that of *Harper* v. *Virginia Board of Education* in which the Court ruled against poll taxes in state elections, not just against payment by those who could not financially afford them. As Marshall stated, ". . . complete impecunity clearly was not determinative of the limits of the disadvantaged class, nor was it essential to make an equal protection claim." That reason could see demonstrated that some individuals were being disadvantaged in this exercise of an implied right was enough for the Court to do away with the state practice. Why not so for property-tax-based financing of public education?

REVIVAL OF SUBSTANTIVE DUE PROCESS

Evidenced in *Rodriguez* is the fact that the Court does not look favorably upon "creation" of a substantive constitutional claim to a right to education even if an individual's financial status is hindering him or her from receiving an adequate education. The Court has also been hesitant to acknowledge a substantive right to welfare benefits, even though principally in *Goldberg* the Court identified such benefits as property. The Court obviously does not look upon property as being absolutely protectable given such later decisions as *Dandridge* and *Jefferson*. One authority finds the possible rebirth of substantive due process offering suggestive support for welfare rights;[7] indeed, he is fearful of the uncertainty of basing welfare claims upon procedural protections which may serve to define these rights in a less liberal way.

In 1857, with Chief Justice Roger B. Taney's morally and practically destructive use of substantive due process in *Dred Scott,* the concept was launched on a long trail of decisions protecting private property holdings against almost any imaginable public-interest claim. These were the years in which the Bill of Rights lay virtually dormant with the Fourteenth Amendment certainly not meeting the usage intended for it by the post-Civil War Congress. The *Lochner* decision is a prime example of the misuse of due process with the Court's deliberate refusal to acknowledge sociological data supporting regulatory state legislation.

Once government benefits became such a pervasive part of American life, the individual's possession of such benefits required legal protection. Since state laws provide first-step procedural guidelines for welfare administration, the level of protection for individual rights may be less than that which a federally enforced substantive due process claim might make. A substantive due process right to welfare can be supported in regard to its social importance and to case precedent. Both conditions are met by an alleged right to welfare since past decisions are numerous in this use of the concept throughout the nineteenth and the first thirty years of the twentieth century. As the demands for government benefits distributed from a community pool increased, the social importance of those qualified asserting their right to benefits became more apparent. If government largess is to serve the public interest, it can do so only in an atmosphere in which the basic right to welfare is realized through the disbursement of benefits that will enhance the opportunity of recipients to better their lot in life.

A RIGHT TO PROCEDURAL DUE PROCESS

Within this intriguing area of legal definition and interpretation, it can also be persuasively argued that procedural due process is as much a right as the claim to government benefits. The *Goldberg* decision saw the Court for the first time perceive welfare benefits as a property right within the context of a procedural due process hearing protecting that right. In effect, the Court made itself the guardian of procedural due process and left to Congress any definitions of substantive due process policy making. This more generous interpretation of welfare rights was made necessary by the development of government benefits becoming so intertwined with personal property that the individual no longer had complete control over the destiny of his or her resources, including employment. In a sense, private property had become a part of the community property pool which was directed by economic fluctuations and government regulations. Consequently, merely labeling welfare benefits as "property" in no way released them from government scrutiny.

The right to a hearing is very directly related to due process, given the essential elements of that procedure including providing the allegedly aggrieved individual with a forum in which all the facts favorable to his or her case may be voiced and considered. As seen above in *Board of Regents of State Colleges* v. *Roth,* the Court interpreted procedural due process as protecting substantive rights independent of the procedures. Associate Justice Stewart, for the majority, ruled that the Fourteenth Amendment procedurally protects property, an interest in which the individual has already established a position. The "entitlement doctrine" was clearly supported therein so that no person can be arbitrarily denied a government benefit for which he or she is eligible.

A THEORY OF JUSTICE: THE JUDICIAL ROLE

Interest in the right-privilege distinction has been reinforced not only by relatively recent Court decisions but also by the publication of Professor John Rawls's *Theory of Justice.* [8] This incredible treatise developed a holistic prescription for society, centered around a "difference principle" which dictates that the distribution of the economic assets within society must be done so as to maximize the position of those who are worst-off in society. Corrective justice must ensue whereby present property holdings are legitimatized, and since fate produces inequalities in wealth, the government must make periodic compensation to the poor in order to enhance their position.

A contrasting view of the distribution of society's wealth is seen through the eyes of Robert Nozick in *Anarchy, State and Utopia.* [9] Professor Nozick disclaims any need for corrective justice in property redistribution beyond those properties acquired by force or fraud. Rawls retorts that no rights, even property rights, should be seen as absolute and beyond government regulation. According to Rawls, all persons have a right to a subsistence livelihood and beyond that, to equal opportunity and freedom from such economic coercion as being forced to take a dangerous job in order to provide for the necessities of life. Furthermore, there is a reciprocal self-interest in having all the members of a society working to their fullest capacity. Once a social consensus as to the basic needs of society is obtained, the judgments of redistribution can be made.

Is it possible to support an "entitlement doctrine" through Rawls's theory? Professor Frank I. Michelman has assumed the quest.[10] The "difference principle" of Professor Rawls implies that each person has the right to a minimum level of such social goods as subsistence, health care, and shelter. Professor Michelman initially suggests that welfare insurance rights can guarantee this Rawlsian provision but finally concludes that while a minimum income may be a natural right, it cannot legitimately be demanded of society by the individual. In other words, society is not obligated to ensure this right. Labeling self-respect as a primary good all people require and thereby using taxation and income transfer to narrow the range of relative deprivation to reinforce self-respect are concepts that may grow out of a theory of insurance rights but, once again, are not guaranteed by society.

Michelman sees Rawls's "opportunity principle" as providing a much more justifiable foundation for the right to welfare than does the "difference principle," since "it seems possible to arrive at somewhat objective and nonrelativistic descriptions of the levels of subsistence, health, and environmental amenity necessary to make persons receptive to educational offerings."[11] The environment through which one receives an education can most assuredly affect the ability of a person to receive training. The "liberty principle" of Rawls's work also reinforces a right to welfare because the enjoyment of educational opportunity is a basic liberty. Finally, within this whole framework, self-respect takes a central role to ensure exercise of the "difference," "opportunity," and "liberty" principles. It is certain " . . . that welfare rights, even those reaching beyond fulfillment of basic wants, also have a role in promoting the self-respect in whose absence the sense of justice will not flourish — the same self-respect, indeed, that the equal liberties are meant to serve."[12]

Michelman holds that the courts must secure the enforcement of substantive constitutional rights even if some equal political liberty may be overriden in the process as the popular legislative will is obstructed. The level of justice must often be considered of higher significance than that of a deficient public will. But these insurance rights will be best assured if at least primary needs are defined within the society's constitution. Judicial review may be called upon to prescribe an administration of welfare rights, but Michelman suggests that the courts may have less faith in the remedial competence of welfare administrators than even school officials (desegregation) or legislators (reapportionment). Can compliance be ensured?

This question is answered by an intriguing thesis under which the judicial perceptions of the day will, to some extent, be conditioned by the popular and legislative sense of justice then in use. Michelman believes that courts do so condition their decisions according to whether or not the legislature is likely to take the initiative in protecting claims to welfare benefits or if it requires some coaxing. He believes that Rawls would agree that such strategy is necessary in the nonideal state. Judges will play a central role in defining positive entitlements from constitutional and statutory law, and consequently

. . . they should conscientiously try to clarify in their own minds some systematic moral theory which justifies and accounts for their decisions, should not shrink from incorporating such thought in their public explanations of what they do, and should be prepared at an appropriate stage in the emergence of a welfare right to declare that such a right exists.[13]

The judicial role is obviously a crucial one in defining the public consciousness and in attempting to enlighten it to higher degrees of human justice. Otherwise, majoritarian emphasis on individual liberty may override the cry of the few for public assistance, even though their condition may be attributable to the economic environment in which they find themselves.

OTHER VIEWS OF THE JUDICIAL ROLE

Not all commentators in the field of administrative law would agree with the Michelman analysis. For instance, Alan Houseman, director of the Research Institute on Legal Assistance of the Legal Services Corporation, contends that explicit legislation is the best protection for the poor;[14] the legislative end based in substantive law must be specific, and the means prescribed for furthering that end. The courts are all too often limited by vague legislation in providing adequate legal protection for the economically disadvantaged.

Of course, the current Supreme Court has been less demanding of legislative means by requiring a legitimate purpose as opposed to the compelling state interest of earlier days. This rationale has largely been developed by the "new majority" of the Court[15] — Justices Stewart, White, Blackmun, and Powell — who tend to agree on the types of legislative classifications that are permissible in welfare cases. These justices will find a closed classification (like that in *Goldberg* v. *Kelly*, where Kelly had no right to a hearing) unacceptable if persons similarly situated are being treated differently or some persons are being totally excluded by an unjustifiable criterion.

The Burger Court has also been more lenient than its predecessor in relying on state administrators to determine the actual implications, especially economic ones, of legislation and court decisions in the welfare area. Although the Burger Court has shown substantial interest in procedural fairness, the Court will rarely question administrative attempts to save money. It is much less likely than its predecessor to embroil itself in administrative particulars in the distribution of limited public resources. This attitude is evident in both the *Dandridge* and *Jefferson* decisions. Yet the Court can be criticized for not acknowledging that procedural fairness and administrative expenditures often walk hand in hand. For instance, in *Goldberg* the Court specified the claimant's right to legal representation but did not require the state to provide it, only to advise on how to retain an attorney from other sources. Given the educational level of many welfare claimants, legal representation is crucial in engendering confidence in the administrative proceedings to which they will be subjected. One author decries the fact that OEO lawyers do not have sufficient time to establish judicially what he calls "the right to life."[16] He contends that "[o]nly the concept of collective bargaining and desegregation affected the lives of as many Americans as would have the 'right to life.'" *Dandridge* was, of course, a major setback in the process. The responsibility now rests with legislative definition, if it is ever to become a reality.

Whether acknowledged by the present Court or not, some legal scholars continue to support the existence of a body of "personal rights" which, although not expressly protected by the Constitution, must receive special judicial attention. Such "implied rights" as voting in state elections, appealing criminal cases, interstate travel, and the rearing of children are prime examples. Justice Marshall used this point as the main thrust of his dissent in the *Rodriguez* decision when he asserted that a quality education is fundamental to effective participation in a liberal democracy even though the right is not expressly granted in the Constitution. Why has the Court recognized other unexpressed rights and refused to acknowledge a protected right to education, housing, and welfare? The majority answered

Justice Marshall by despairing of the possibility of involving itself in the intricacies of administrative decision making regarding the financing of public education. The issue has been left unanswered.

Constitutional scholar Henry J. Abraham, in agreeing with the *Rodriguez* majority, has questioned the advisability of viewing the obviously desirable concepts of "freedom from want," "equalization of wealth," and "economic independence" as constitutionally guaranteed.[17] Professor Abraham's point is thoughtful, but there are no Supreme Court decisions involving proposals of equalizing wealth. The Court, however, has clearly specified that the government cannot be arbitrary in its actions even if the perceived substantive right of some is uncertain. The abandonment of the "right-privilege" distinction does not foretell the termination of procedural due process. In the words of one scholar, the Court has come to realize ". . . that the 'right' to own property or the 'right' to work in the private sector is necessarily subject to public regulation compatible with some minimum standard of substantive due process; however, the Court had never asserted that such an interest was wholly outside the protection of the due process clause."[18]

Procedural due process requires that a fair hearing of claims concerning a person's alleged right to act in a certain way or to collect a benefit be held to determine if such a right has been erroneously claimed. In turn, equal protection of the laws protects a person from being treated arbitrarily by the denial of a benefit because of the classification into which he or she is unreasonably placed. Thus, equal protection of the laws can restrain the state from arbitrary action in regard to unexpressed rights as well as such clearly protected ones as freedom of speech and the free exercise of religion. It is important to note that the landmark decision in *Brown* v. *Board of Education* did not discuss the "right" to quality education but indirectly protected this societal advantage by declaring racial segregation of the public schools to violate equal protection of the laws. In this way, a "right" not specifically recognized by the Court found itself reinforced nevertheless.

3

PROCEDURAL DUE PROCESS
IN THE BURGER COURT

The 1970s proved to be a critical decade in the development of judicial thought regarding administrative obligations to protect the constitutional rights of welfare recipients. In the early years of the decade, the United States Supreme Court was especially eager to see these rights maintained, even considering the continually crucial issue of tolerable administrative costs. The tension between financial considerations and the individual's interest in basic survival can cause an administrative hearing quickly to develop an adversarial atmosphere rather than one of cooperation, with the balance drawn by the presiding ALJ (administrative law judge). One commentator has stated that ". . . to the extent to which the administrative apparatus and the welfare recipients share the same goals, an environment for fairness may exist."[1] The burden on the ALJ is obvious. A mistake in decision making will almost surely result in dire economic consequences for the claimant since, by law, persons living on welfare benefits have no other sources of revenue available to them. Therefore, even recoupment of funds may fall short of remedying the damage done by the termination of welfare payments. Such a person is obviously placed at the mercy of administrative decision makers and may not even be able to participate in a hearing to rectify the sitation, having to be more concerned with finding a source for the family's meals the next day.

Statistics demonstrate that AFDC (Aid to Families with Dependent Children) hearings are a rare occurrence in many states. A survey of forty-nine states and the District of Columbia in July 1975[2] showed a mean of 1,422 hearings requested per month from January to June 1975. The standard deviation was 5,428 with a minimum of 0 and a maximum of 36,369. New York State provided the maximum, California (with 9,856 hearings requested) being second. Only five other states fall into the range between 4,000 and 1,000, with thirty-one states falling below 500. The same study demonstrated a mean ratio of only .009 between the number of requests for a hearing in that same time period and the number of AFDC applications plus monthly ongoing AFDC cases. Combining AFDC and Medical Assistance hearing requests, the study showed that a mean of 30.2 percent of hearings among forty-four responses was resolved in favor of the claimant with a range of 0 percent to 66.1 percent. Considering the disparity in hearing procedures among the states, it is perhaps surprising that this range is not even greater.

THE BEGINNING OF STANDARDS: A RIGHT TO BE HEARD

In June 1969, just a few months before Warren Burger assumed his position as chief justice of the Supreme Court, the Court heard the case of *Sniadach* v. *Family Finance Corporation of Bay View* involving a garnishment law in the state of Wisconsin. The statute was held to violate due process of law under the Fourteenth Amendment on the ground that it did not provide advance notice of the action to the garnishee nor opportunity to be heard prior to the seizure of wages. The majority opinion saw no state interest being served by these drastic procedures and concluded that the family's economic condition was of primary importance. By requiring prior notice and a hearing of some sort before administrative action is taken because of the basic nature of the proposed deprivation, the Court set the stage for its consideration of AFDC hearings.

Before the Court began establishing standards for welfare hearings, the states had no procedural guidelines other than those in the form of the Department of Health, Education and Welfare's regulations. In the late 1960s, these required an informal conference between the claimant and the caseworker before benefits were terminated.[3] In July 1970, a new regulation was put into effect whereby benefits were to be continued until a decision was forthcoming from a fair hearing in which an appointed attorney was assured.[4] Consequently, the Court, upon hearing *Goldberg* v. *Kelly* in October 1969, and knowing the new regulation was in the offing, was in a position merely to dismiss or remand the case for implementation of the new HEW regulation. However, because of the variety of modes in utilizing federal regulations followed by the various states, the Court did rightly in addressing the constitutional questions raised.

THE GOLDBERG v. KELLY DECISION

Justice William Brennan, writing for a majority of five in *Goldberg* v. *Kelly,* laid down basic procedural standards for the conducting of all AFDC hearings involving the termination of public welfare benefits. In many ways, the specificity of the decision is reminiscent of the famous *Miranda* ruling, in which Chief Justice Earl Warren essentially placed himself in the role of a national police chief. In the present case, the state of New York, through its General Home Relief Program, already provided a system whereby the claimant was informed by his or her caseworker of any proposed termination of benefits and that he or she could submit a written statement to the supervisor who would make the final decision prior to the possible cutoff of benefits. If an adverse decision was forthcoming, the claimant could then request a hearing before an independent state hearing officer at which he or she could appear, give oral testimony, question adverse witnesses, and receive a record of the proceedings. The United States Supreme Court, however, found these procedures inadequate to meet the due process requirements of Fourteenth Amendment. Justice Brennan was unwilling to avoid the constitutional issue at hand.

In balancing the need of the welfare recipient against the interests of the state, Justice Brennan found the former far weightier. He was concerned with the possibility of a citizen's being left destitute after having been made to believe he or she was eligible for government benefits. Not only do these benefits provide for those in impoverished circumstances; they also offer hope for escape from them, which would, of course, benefit the whole society.

The specific due process requirements of a given case will thus, according to the Court, depend upon the degree of loss imposed on the claimant. Only in cases of a "pressing public interest" may government benefits be terminated without a prior hearing, as in seizing food that is offered for sale but is unsafe for human consumption. But when welfare is discontinued, the very survival of a family is at stake. Government financial interests cannot be the first concern in such a situation.

Justice Brennan asserted that "rudimentary due process" would be sufficient in welfare administration, given the need for a rapid resolution of the eligibility issue, the informality of the administrative process as contrasted with the criminal justice system, and the overwhelming case loads of many welfare departments. He emphasized that he did not wish to impose strict federal standards of procedure upon state administrators, and that the "fair hearing" stipulations of the HEW statute would suffice but must be followed. According to the Court majority, "the fundamental requisite of due process of law is the opportunity to be heard."[5] The Court then, in some detail, discussed the standards that must be met in order for the claimant to secure a meaningful hearing. Essentially, these are ". . . timely and adequate notice detailing the reasons for a proposed termination, and an effective opportunity to defend by confronting any adverse witnesses and by presenting his own arguments and evidence orally."

The right to be heard entails administrative notice that probably should include a letter and personal conference with the caseworker, as the state of New York had already provided. The capabilities of the recipient must determine what procedures are guaranteed; this is especially pertinent in dealing with welfare claimants who may have had little opportunity to obtain training in effectively expressing themselves. New York's procedures violated due process by not allowing the recipient to be present at the hearing, with an attorney if he or she wishes, in order to present evidence and cross-examine adverse witnesses. A mere written submission by the recipient, to be reviewed by the hearing examiner, does not permit any oral explanation which may be more representative of the recipient's case. The government must make its own file on the case available to the claimant so that he or she may meet the issues directly.[6]

The hearing officer must be impartial, basing his or her decision on the legal rules and evidence of the hearing. In fact, he or she should make plain the reasons for the decision and the evidence used to support it. While the decision maker may have had some prior involvement in the case at hand, he or she should not have had any part in the previous determination to discontinue benefits.

The majority opinion in *Goldberg* is remarkable in that while it establishes explicit due process requirements for the states, it also recognizes that each state must be given some latitude in meeting its own peculiar circumstances. Acknowledging that it was dealing with administrative hearings and not a criminal courtroom proceeding, the Court was lenient on some points. For instance, it did not specify what "timely and adequate notice" must be; it merely made some suggestions as to what it *might* be, considering some welfare recipients' educational limitations. The "right to be heard" is indeed basic to this whole process, but the Court did not set rigid requirements for all cases to guarantee it. Again, given the personal capabilities of some recipients, the assistance of an attorney may be crucial to the meaningful exercise of this right, but not necessarily in every case.[7] No particular order of proof or evidence must be followed, although all claimants should, at some point, have the opportunity to present oral evidence in their own behalf. The hearing examiner does not necessarily have to keep a complete record of the proceedings or make a comprehensive decision as in a criminal proceeding; the degree of completeness is a matter of individual discretion.[8]

Dissenting in *Goldberg* and its companion case, *Wheeler* v. *Montgomery*,[9] were two justices who often found themselves on opposite sides of an issue: Associate Justice Hugo Black and Chief Justice Warren Burger. In this instance, they were joined by Associate Justice Potter Stewart. Justice Black discussed the burden that welfare places on the nation and the deceitfulness of ineligible recipients. He, and Burger with him, contended that the Court majority had devised its own particular interpretation of what "fair and humane procedure" in a welfare hearing should be, rather than recognizing that there are no absolute standards of fairness to meet all situations. Justice Black argued that the majority failed to understand that due process must ". . . mean something definite and have an explicit content." He saw the Court as imposing its own inflexible, historically conditioned perspective upon this constitutional precept rather than just accepting it as a general principle, subject to varied interpretations and meant to control government. What is to stop the Court from next deciding that welfare benefits may not be stopped until a judicial review is made of the administrative decision? Black argued that the Court must leave Congress and the state legislatures much more room for experimentation within their own socioeconomic environments.

Chief Justice Burger held that the courts should have been willing to allow the new HEW regulations to take effect and not force its unnecessary interpretation of due process on the states. He was also critical that the majority did not make itself clear as to whether the *Goldberg* requirements would apply to reductions in benefits[10] and denial of increases as well as to initial applications or requests for special assistance.

BEYOND GOLDBERG

The right to be heard prior to a deprivation by the state was again put before the Court in 1972 in *Fuentes* v. *Shevin* when the justices looked at the constitutionality of Florida's replevin statute. This law provided that a private party could obtain a prejudgment writ of replevin from a court clerk by posting a bond double the value of property to be seized. The sheriff would then execute the writ and hold the property for three days in which time the defendant could reclaim it by posting a double-value bond. By a 4-3 vote the Court ruled that the Florida statute violated Fourteenth Amendment due process because it did not provide for prior notice of the state's action. Justice Stewart, for the slim majority, asserted that prior notice and a hearing must be granted before a state deprived a person of his or her private property. Otherwise, the full weight of a wrong decision could not be undone. Such action prior to notice and hearing can be justified only ". . . where some valid governmental interest is at stake that justifies postponing the hearing until after the event."[11] Of course, in this case it was not the government itself laying claim to private property but rather a creditor of the appellant. Justice Stewart rejected Florida's claim that the bond would prevent abuse; rather he made the assumption that most uneducated people are unlikely to challenge the action. Neither would the possibly "temporary" nature of the situation justify it. As in *Sniadach, Bell,* and *Goldberg,* the Court majority would not justify the state's depriving the individual of his or her property without a prior hearing, even when in *Bell* and *Goldberg* the property took the form of government benefits. Justice White, joined by Chief Justice Burger and Justice Blackmun, dissented on the ground that a seller also loses in a repossession and is therefore unlikely to be in error in claiming a right to repossession.

Approximately two years later, Justice Rehnquist, writing for another narrow majority, held for the Court in *Arnett* v. *Kennedy* that a federal employee does not have the right to a trial-type hearing and an impartial adjudicator prior to the termination of employment. He wrote:

The types of "liberty" and "property" protected by the Due Process Clause vary widely, and what may be required under that Clause in dealing with one set of interests which it protects may not be required in dealing with another set of interests.

Consequently, Justice Rehnquist was able to distinguish this case from those such as *Goldberg, Fuentes, Bell,* and *Sniadach.* He relied heavily upon the *Roth* decision to support the procedures of the Office of Economic Opportunity and the Civil Service Commission in their treatment of Arnett. Under these procedures, the decision of termination of employment had been made by the official bringing the charges, but Arnett had been given notice of the impending decision and an opportunity to argue against its merits after his termination. Rehnquist upheld 5 U.S.C., Section 7501, a section of the Lloyd-La Follette Act, providing that "[e]xamination of witnesses, trial, or hearing is not required but may be provided in the discretion of the individual directing the removal or suspension without pay."

Under Section 7511 of the act, Arnett was defined as a "preference eligible," meaning that he had passed a probationary period of employment and was therefore "protected" under Section 7512 of the act. It provided him with thirty days' advance written notice, reasonable time to answer charges in writing and with affidavits, and notice of an adverse decision. Under the act, having been removed ". . . only for such cause as will promote the efficiency of the service" (Sections 7501, 7512), he had not availed himself of his right to respond to the notice of adverse action nor to the agency's invitation to review adverse materials in his file. Justice Rehnquist was satisfied that an evidentiary, trial-type hearing was available to Arnett under Civil Service Commission regulations upon appeal after dismissal and that upon reinstatement, back pay would be awarded. Obviously, a very different mentality was at work in *Arnett* than was evidenced in *Goldberg.* Government employment was certainly not taking the form of a property claim; nor was the Court making any effort to balance the destitution that might be caused by a wrongful termination of employment against the administrative inconvenience caused by holding a hearing.

DISABILITY: A LESSER NEED?

In the area of disability hearings, the Burger Court made several basic procedural distinctions from welfare hearings, even though both were administered through the auspices of the Department of Health, Education, and Welfare. The first of these cases — *Richardson* v. *Perales* — was decided in May 1971; it revolved around the issues of whether when a physician himself was not present at the hearing, his written report was admissible as evidence, and similarly whether the testimony of a physician who had not examined the claimant but was acting as an adviser to the hearing examiner was admissible. The claimant charged that the evidence of both physicians was hearsay and objected to not having the opportunity to cross-examine either of them. The United States Court of Appeals had held that since the claimant had not requested subpoenas for these witnesses, he himself had negated his right to cross-examination. The reports, although hearsay, were therefore admissible even if they did not constitute "substantial evidence."

The Supreme Court reversed and remanded. Justice Blackmun wrote the majority opinion in which he distinguished the rules of evidence followed in a court of law from those used in an administrative proceeding. He asserted that strict rules of evidence are not necessary in the latter instance; the hearing examiner should set the mode of these informal proceedings. He further stated that the hearings ". . . should be liberal and not strict in tone and operation. This is the obvious intent of Congress so long as the procedures are fundamentally fair." In defining "substantial evidence," Justice Blackmun held it to be ". . . such relevant evidence as a reasonable mind might accept as adequate to support a conclusion."[12] The Court held that written reports made by physicians who have examined the claimant constitute "substantial evidence" when the claimant has not asked for a subpoena to secure their oral testimony, even though it is also hearsay in that cross-examination is impossible.

The Court also backed the hearing examiner's use of a medical adviser to clarify complex medical information. Although this indeed might be hearsay evidence, it is acceptable as long as it is relevant to the case at hand under the dictates of both the Social Security Act and the Administrative Procedures Act.[13] Neither is there an imbalance toward support of the government's case when the hearing examiner who is to decide the validity of the claim also acts as a fact gatherer as long as he or she is not acting as counsel. The Social Security Administration's reversal rate on state denials of disability claims is an impressive 44.2 percent, attesting to the fairness of the system, according to Justice Blackmun.

Justice Douglas, joined by Justices Black and Brennan, wrote a seething dissent in which he asserted that the written reports of doctors who in some cases have not even examined the claimants should not be used as "substantial evidence" without cross-examination. The dissenters were especially concerned about the testimony of a medical adviser, who was obviously in a position where he or she could influence the hearing examiner's decision, being admissible without the expert's having been subject to cross-examination.

In another significant disability insurance case, *Mathews* v. *Eldridge,* the Supreme Court differentiated between disability payments and welfare benefits by asserting that the termination of the former need not be preceded by an evidentiary hearing. In deciding against continued eligibility, the local agency decision for termination is to be sent to the Social Security Agency in its region; if the SSA agrees with the local decision, it in turn will send the beneficiary a letter giving its reasons for the decision and notice of the right of the beneficiary to ask for reconsideration. The beneficiary may then seek an evidentiary hearing before an SSA administrative-law judge and may also subsequently appeal beyond that level to the SSA Appeals Council and then to judicial review. At any stage, a favorable opinion for the beneficiary will result in retroactive benefits. In this particular case, however, Mr. Eldridge had sought a judicial remedy immediately after initial denial, seeking a major change in the administrative review system.

Associate Justice Powell, writing the opinion for the majority of six, stated that "a claim to a predeprivation hearing as a matter of constitutional right rests on the proposition that full relief cannot be obtained at a postdeprivation hearing." Thus, the chance of retroactive benefit payments weighed heavily in the reasoning of the Court. While Justice Powell was willing to acknowledge the receipt of benefits as a "property interest" within Fifth Amendment due process of law, he emphasized, as the Court had in earlier decisions, that the particular circumstances of each case determine what the due process requirements in effect will be. Powell specified that due process requires a consideration of (1) the private interest affected, (2) the "risk of an erroneous deprivation," using the established procedures, and (3) the government's financial and administrative burden. All these considerations must be balanced against one another in the case decision at hand.

The beneficiary has a continual burden to demonstrate his or her eligibility for disability benefits since the Social Security disability program requires a person demonstrate inability to be gainfully employed for a year's time only for the initial administrative determination.[14] This is done through medical diagnosis. If the current receiver of benefits is found to be no longer disabled, via a medical examination by an independent consulting physician to the state agency, the claimant may begin the appeals process. During a nonadversarial evidentiary hearing before an administrative-law judge (ALJ), the claimant may be represented by an attorney whereas the SSA is not.

The Supreme Court in *Eldridge* distinguished between the need for welfare payments and those for disability. The weight of need probably will not be as great with the latter since the beneficiary may have other sources of income through family members, worker's compensation, savings, or insurance. On the other hand, legally to receive welfare benefits requires that a person be destitute of any other means of support. Consequently, an erroneous administrative decision to terminate welfare payments will be far more crucial to the continued well-being of the claimant and his or her family. Also, eligibility for welfare is more difficult to ascertain than disability, which is based on medical reports. Even though there is no legal definition of "disability," the standards are somewhat more exacting than in the case of welfare, which is more likely to require a hearing to get to the intricacies of the situation. A hearing may also be more applicable to welfare claims, since many welfare recipients would find submitting written reports a difficult avenue by which to voice their arguments; a nonadversarial, "conversational" hearing might well be more conducive to getting at the facts. In disability claims, the written reports of physicians play a central role in the decision-making process.

The public interest of avoiding unnecessary hearings and the continuance of undeserved benefits weighed heavily in Justice Powell's decision. The recovery of undeserved benefits is always uncertain. Therefore, in balancing all interests involved, the Court found it must put some faith in the judgment of SSA administrators who have undoubtedly developed some level of expertise in assessing the validity of disability claims. Justices Brennan and Marshall, the dissenters, however, were unwilling to place that much faith in administrative decisions which might lead to erroneous deprivations of benefits. They found the Court's argument of lesser deprivation in the case of disability as opposed to welfare unconvincing since the other forms of possible assistance are unknown in the situation of the individual disability recipient.

Two relatively recent United States District Court decisions have dealt with the procedural nature of disability hearings before ALJs (administrative-law judges). In March 1977, the U.S. District Court for the District of Maryland ruled in *Roe* v. *Califano* that the presence of counsel representing the claimant is not required to make a disability hearing "full and fair." The district judge held that ". . . it is only in those cases when there is a showing of prejudice that the question of lack of counsel may warrant a finding of unfairness." In the present cases, he believed that the plaintiff had been able to present his claim orally and in writing in an acceptable manner without the need for counsel. He rested his decision upon his interpretation of *Perales.* Approximately one month later, the United States District Court of Appeals for the Southern District of New York held in *Lupinacei* v. *Mathews* that ALJs must make inquiries into the plaintiff's ability to work despite his or her medical condition. In other words, the ALJ should not merely assume that in and of itself the claimant's condition is disabling. The district court judge held that this obligation ". . . is especially compelling where a claimant is not represented by counsel and lacks familiarity with legal and administrative proceedings. . . ." Although counsel is not required at such hearings, the ALJ must play the dual role of protecting the plaintiff's right to a fair presentation of his or her claim as well as the government's right to assess eligibility for benefits.

The Supreme Court has obviously not been persuaded to extend the *Goldberg* procedures wholesale to the area of Social Security claims under federal Old-Age, Survivors, and Disability Insurance Benefits (OASDI).[15] With *Perales,* the central issue of cross-examination of adverse witnesses saw welfare claims placed on a higher level of protection than those of disability. In *Eldridge,* a pretermination evidentiary hearing of any sort was said not to be necessary in disability cases. In the latter decision, the Court made clear what its reasoning had been in avoiding the constitutional claims in *Richardson* v. *Wright* in 1972. In that case, the Court rejected a claim for a pretermination evidentiary hearing, stating that it wished to allow the Secretary of the Department of Health, Education and Welfare a chance to implement new regulations providing the beneficiary with notice of a proposed suspension of disability benefits and an opportunity to respond in writing. Justices Douglas and Brennan, dissenting, argued that there was no reason for the Court to defer to agency regulations here when it had not done so in *Goldberg.* Obviously, the Court was unwilling to extend specific due process requirements to Social Security benefits. In its handling of an unemployment compensation case,[16] the Court also declined to extend the rigidities of adequate notice and an evidentiary hearing to the termination of these benefits.

In *Goldberg,* the Court required an evidentiary hearing with specific due process provisions in situations where "brutal need" *and* disputed questions of fact could be demonstrated. A strong argument can be presented that the need of a large number of Social Security beneficiaries is critical to basic existence. Furthermore it might be argued that in *Wright* the Court was in error in seeing the disability as an objective consideration. Indeed, there is no legal definition of "disability," and many disputed facts may therefore come to bear on the decision-making process. Doctors do not always agree on a diagnosis, and a claimant's education and work history will have much to do with his or her capacity to secure employment. Furthermore, the veracity of the testimony of all witnesses is not a certainty.[17] Thus, a hearing may be crucial to resolving these issues. In his dissenting opinion in *Wright,* Justice Brennan noted the impressive reversal rate (55 percent) of claimants appealing termination of their disability benefits at the hearing level.[18] This in itself questions the objectivity of such considerations. Yet the Burger Court has been unwilling to demand that the specific due process requirements of *Goldberg* be used in hearings determining the continued receipt of other forms of government benefits. Realistically, the levels of need among beneficiaries of these various programs may be similar, but the Court has been unwilling to establish the formula to assess need and the procedural requirements necessary to meet it in all programs. Also in the area of AFDC home visitation, the Court has left actual procedural determinations largely to state administrators.

Besides the consideration of what is a legally correct hearing to determine continued eligibility for public-assistance payments, the Court has also been asked to rule upon proper administrative procedures in conducting visits to the home of welfare recipients. This is obviously an area that might permit much administrative abuse of the privacy of the home.

The frequency of home visits varies greatly from one state to another. A recent study indicates that an approximation of the percentage of AFDC applicants receiving home visits rests at a mean of 67 percent with thirty-seven states responding; the range was from 3 to 100 percent;[19] A brief look at some of the Supreme Court's earlier decisions in the relatively unexplored area of administrative searches and seizures will provide the background for the Burger Court's more recent decisions in the field.

INSPECTIONS ARE SEARCHES

In 1950, in *District of Columbia* v. *Little,* the Supreme Court heard a case involving the refusal of entry to a health officer who without a warrant was responding to complaints about health conditions in a private home. The majority of six refused to meet the constitutional issue and merely held that Ms. Little's complaining and criticizing, as opposed to threatening, did not constitute an interference with the inspection in any real sense. She, therefore, was not liable to prosecution. The two dissenters, Justices Burton and Reed, addressing the more substantial constitutional issue, argued that the Fourth Amendment provision against unreasonable searches and seizures does not require a search warrant in this instance since the means used by the inspector ". . . were of such a reasonable, general, routine, accepted and important character. . . ." Consequently, the respondent's action was interference with a legal administrative action. Some Supreme Court observers might argue that even supposedly "reasonable" administrative action may violate the basic constitutional rights of individual persons, but the majority, headed by Justice Black, chose not to address the issue.

Two cases of precedence – *Camara* v. *Municipal Court of the City and County of San Francisco* and *See* v. *City of Seattle* – came to the Court seventeen years later. Herein, the urgency of protecting the public health and safety came into play but was not controlling. In *Camara*, the appellant had refused to permit a warrantless search of his private residence as provided in the Housing Code of the Public Health Department of the City of San Francisco. Justice White, writing the opinion for the majority of six, held that the Court was unwilling to accept the position that only if an individual is suspected of criminal behavior is he or she to receive constitutional protection. He noted that when an inspector enters a home without a warrant, the private citizen has no way of knowing if such a search is required, if the inspector is acting within lawful limits and with proper authority. It is the private citizen who must assume the risk of punishment in refusing entry. Therefore, White concluded, a disinterested party must decide on the need for the search once it has been refused. He stated that ". . . broad statutory safeguards are no substitute for individualized review, particularly when those safeguards may only be invoked at the risk of a criminal penalty."[19]

The majority did not view the need to protect the public health and safety as skewing the balance away from protection of the individual, since the Court was not advocating the complete elimination of all health inspections; it was only placing a procedural requirement upon them. This requirement might be based upon nothing more than sufficient time having passed to warrant an inspection. In fact, as a practical matter, warrants should be sought for searches of single locations only after entry had been refused. White emphasized that nothing in the Court's decision should be construed to mean that area searches may be conducted in the public interest without warrants or that prompt, warrantless action may not be justifiable in such cases as the possible sale of contaminated food or the need for a health quarantine.

In the *See* decision, the Court dealt with a private citizen's refusal to allow a warrantless search of his commercial warehouse by the Seattle Fire Department. The city demonstrated an intention to obtain a subpoena for certain corporate books and records within the warehouse, and this the Court majority found to be a persuasive factor. The subpoena would provide the proper guidelines for the search, i.e., a limited scope, a relevant purpose, and a specific direction. Furthermore, the subpoenaed party could obtain judicial review of the reasonableness of the search before suffering a penalty for noncompliance. The reasonableness of each search must be considered on a case-by-case basis, according to the majority opinion of the justices. In this case, the fire department was conducting a routine, citywide canvass.

In both *Camara* and *See,* the Court emphasized the need for a reasonable motivation lying behind any administrative search and the opportunity for judicial review before any penalties were placed upon the refusing party. But through these decisions, a *nonrefused* warrantless search is legal as long as ensuing criminal prosecution is not possible.

A classic case of administrative abuse in this area came out of California in 1967 in *Parrish* v. *The Civil Service Commission of the County of Alameda.* The state supreme court was faced with a fact-situation in which an Alameda County social worker had been discharged for his refusal, based on constitutional grounds, to participate in an early morning mass raid on the private homes of welfare recipients. The purpose of the raids was to locate "unauthorized males" living in these homes – in other words, unreported persons not eligible to benefit from the receipt of welfare.[20] The amount of benefits given a child under AFDC was computed by the state according to the presence or absence of such males. Admittedly, most of the homes searched were not even under suspicion as to the eligibility of the occupants for benefits. The social workers had been instructed to work in pairs, one entering through the back door after his companion had received access through the front door. Then the entire house was to be searched. The raids were labeled "Operation Bedcheck." With the sanction of having their welfare cut off, most beneficiaries were forced into compliance.

The California Supreme Court held these raids to be a violation of the Fourth Amendment, because misrepresentation regarding eligibility for welfare benefits is a crime. The Court also was concerned over the "loose" correlation of the means used to meet the end of discovering welfare fraud; at least half of the homes had been selected at random with no evidence of fraud available. Finally, the Court relied somewhat upon the *Griswold* decision to demonstrate that welfare recipients have a right to privacy within their own homes as do all other citizens.

The *Parrish* decision was not, however, persuasive when the United States Supreme Court encountered the same constitutional issue four years later in *Wyman* v. *James*. The Court then refused to rely on the *Sherbert* ruling that a person cannot be forced to waive one constitutional right in order to exercise his or her right to receive government benefits for which he or she is eligible. In other words, the Court did not want to resurrect the right-privilege distinction it had resolved in *Goldberg* and which had been a strong argument for the state court in *Parrish*.

INVESTIGATION AND/OR REHABILITATION

In *Wyman* v. *James,* the United States Supreme Court was asked to meet the constitutional issue of a New York State AFDC recipient's refusal to submit to a visit to her home by a caseworker. She had been notified of the impending visit several days before it was to occur; Ms. James' response was that she would be glad to supply additional information relevant to her need for public assistance but would not permit the visit. Consequently, her benefits were terminated pursuant to New York law, although she was not liable to criminal prosecution for her refusal, as in *Camara*.

Justice Blackmun, writing for a majority of five — and of six in part — held that these visits or "contacts" with recipients served both a "rehabilitative" and "investigative" purpose. He saw nothing unreasonable, under Fourth Amendment provisions, in this administrative action. In fact, Justice Blackmun emphasized that the New York State Department of Social Services was not conducting a criminal investigation in such home visits, and therefore no searches and seizures within the context of the Fourth Amendment could occur. Requiring that a search warrant be issued before such a visit would imply criminal conduct. How could the caseworker realistically establish probable cause on the need to see a particular child prior to the visit? Yet Justice Blackmun showed concern for the protection of children in a welfare home, stating that part of the reason for home visits is to see that the dependent children are receiving proper care. If neglect can be demonstrated, criminal prosecution may ensue. One must ask whether Justice Blackmun was assuming that children in welfare homes are more likely to be abused or can we assume that all homes are subject to similar warrantless inspections? And if the children's benefit is of primary concern, can we assume that they will be benefited by the termination of welfare payments?[21]

The Court majority of five thus held that home visits of AFDC recipients by caseworkers are not searches within the definition of the Fourth Amendment. Justice White then concurred with the Court, although believing that these visits are searches. Even so, the Court majority held such visits are not unreasonable as long as written notice is given several days in advance and the privacy of the recipient is emphasized in the visit. The visits are only to serve the purpose of verifying the residence of a child (i.e., continued eligibility) and perhaps impending medical need. In the final analysis, they are not forced upon the recipient, and no criminal penalties will be incurred if the visit is refused. The welfare benefits will simply be terminated, and a post-termination hearing can be held to justify this action.

Justice Blackmun emphasized that the state has the obligation to guard against welfare fraud and thereby assure the American public of the proper use of these governmental funds. In fact, the justice hinged the majority opinion upon this consideration as opposed to arguments that home visits are essentially ineffective in verifying eligibility. An amicus curiae brief had been submitted to the Court by the Social Service Employees' Union, Local 371, arguing the ineffectiveness of home visits based upon factors such as understaffing, rapid turnover, and heavy case loads. Any rehabilitation during home visits under these circumstances would be highly unlikely, as well as assuring eligibility. This "ad hoc balancing" between administrative necessity and individual rights basically allows the Court to do whatever it wishes. Such constitutional inconsistencies as a warrantless search and criminal prosecution for the felony of child abuse are the result of this reasoning. With such a possibility, ". . . no less than full probable cause to search should be tolerated."[22] Getting a warrant after refusal and with some evidence of such activity should not be difficult.

The dissenters in *Wyman* obviously had reason to question the validity of the majority's thinking. Justice Douglas asserted that New York

State cannot "buy up" the personal rights guaranteed by the Constitution with government largess. Douglas argued that two standards of justice were evident in the majority opinion: one for welfare recipients who are targets for administrative abuse; the other for private business subsidized by government largess that need not submit to such incursions. Also in dissent, Justices Marshall and Brennan noted the *Camara* decision in which they felt the Court had rejected the reasoning that the Fourth Amendment protects only suspected criminals. And even if the Fourth Amendment be considered so restricted, an AFDC caseworker's "visit" may result in civil penalty and even criminal conviction for fraud. No federal regulations require that such visits be made to support continued eligibility, and examples of doling out other government benefits demonstrate that review of public records, expenditure receipts, and nonhome interviews are often adequate to establish eligibility. Justice Marshall, who wrote the opinion, rejected the notion of the supposed paternalism of the welfare caseworker in assisting the rehabilitation of welfare recipients by these visits. Rather, he asserted, quoting *Goldberg,* "Relevant constitutional restraints apply as much to the withdrawal of public assistance benefits as to disqualification for unemployment compensation, . . . denial of a tax exemption, . . . or discharge from public employment " (Goldberg v. Kelly, 397 U.S. 254, 262 [1970]).

The Supreme Court followed suit in its next term in *U.S.* v. *Biswell.* Under the Gun Control Act of 1968,[23] the respondent was licensed to keep and sell sporting weapons in his pawnshop. An inspection of the shop resulted in the seizure, without warrant, of two illegally sawed-off rifles. The Burger Court held that no unauthorized force had been used in this situation; indeed, "[t]he lawfulness of the search does not depend upon consent." If this federal statute is to be enforced, the Court majority argued, inspections without warrants are necessary. As long as the Court sees such inspections as meeting the reasonable requirements of narrowly drawn statutory law, it will not interfere with administrative discretion in applying the statute if the actions taken are reasonable. In fact, ever since the *Goldberg* decision, the Court has consistently been willing to pay such deference.[24]

ARGUMENTS ABOUT ADMINISTRATIVE "VISITS"

Academic reaction to the *Wyman* decision was skeptical for, as far back as 1963, Professor Charles Reich had enunciated the potential dangers of "welfare raids" in a now often-quoted article.[25] Professor Reich, interpreting from previous judicial decisions, wrote that one or more of three conditions must be met for welfare home visitation to be constitutional: (1) the recipient's consent, expressed or implied; (2) the object of the search is not to secure evidence for criminal prosecution or forfeiture; and (3) the search itself is reasonable. In regard to consent, Reich was quick to note that the mere authority of government officials may coerce consent without the beneficiary knowing whether he or she has the right to refuse. The beneficiary may also falsely assume that by having received benefits, he or she has implied consent to such searches, whereas Professor Reich's well-known labeling of government largess as property once it has been received pressed him to assert that such a receipt cannot be so conditioned.

The reason for the search must not be connected with possible criminal prosecution which misrepresentation in welfare eligibility can bring. Furthermore, Reich was willing to go one step beyond this point to contend that the Fourth Amendment surely includes evidence that will cause forfeitures as well as criminal convictions. He was more "liberal" also than the current Court in noting that generally searches not incident to a lawful arrest have required warrants. Reich was concerned for the balance of protection to weigh in favor of the recipient of largess since welfare dependents can easily be intimidated by governmental tactics and are unlikely to question their administrators. He pointed to Section 2236 of Title 18, U.S.C., which forbids the search of private homes by any federal employee administering any federal statute. Neither should federal authorities condone abusive state action by such visits.

Shortly before *Wyman* was decided by the Supreme Court, legal commentators began anticipating the decision. Justice Blackmun was supported by some who concurred that such visits should be looked upon as having a "service orientation" as provided by the 1956 Amendment to the Social Security Act. One legal authority distinguished welfare benefits from social security programs by writing the following:

While social insurance is geared to the average needs of large numbers of people, public assistance is directed to the peculiar needs of individuals whose financial dependence is supposedly caused by personal inadequacies rather than by general social or economic flaws.[26]

Of course, the attribution of poverty to "personal inadequacies" is open to argument;[27] the commentator, however, is undoubtedly correct in noting that each case requires knowledge of a particular home environment. Accordingly, there is not necessarily an adversarial atmosphere created by the gaining of this knowledge; "thus verifying eligibility is simply the obverse of ensuring that the client has all he is entitled to receive, and information gathered for either purpose is helpful for recommending social services."[28]

Justice Blackmun also received support for his argument that a warrant is not appropriate to a welfare visit since the visit is primarily made as a service to the recipient. Neither could the caseworker be expected to have as much information about the recipient's home situation prior to the visit. This same supporter of Justice Blackmun advocated the "separation of eligibility determination and service in welfare administration" so that caseworkers are oriented only toward service to the client. It was hoped that eligibility standards could be made more standard so that clerical personnel could initially handle these determinations. Then warrants would be necessary only on eligibility inquiries, and lawyers could represent clients under question during office interviews.[29] The present writer finds these recommendations imaginative and feasible and wishes that Justice Blackmun might have made a similar suggestion. However, once again, the Burger Court proved that it was unlikely to replace the judgment of state welfare administrators with its own, even when such a practical suggestion might resolve a basic constitutional issue. Caseworkers acting to serve, not prosecute, recipients would be able to communicate with recipients more effectively, even to the point of making them more self-assured of their economic condition.[30]

The Court has obviously not set clear standards for administrative visits. One suggested approach from academic circles has been that rather than merely assessing the need for a warrant before an administrative inspection, the decision should be ". . . *based on a certain standard of probable cause*" in each individual case. If, for instance, the inspection was instigated by a complaint, a warrant would be necessary. But if the visit was purely routine, no warrant would be needed. "Warrantless inspections of a very small category of highly regulated businesses, such as those dealing in firearms, food, drugs and liquor, should be permissible because there is in fact little expectation of privacy in the carrying on of such businesses." A "lesser" probable-cause standard would require a warrant for even routine inspections of homes and code inspections of business premises.[31] An opportunity to refuse agency inspection must be given. Also to be considered is the possibility of obtaining the information sought in the inspection by other means. For instance, in welfare cases, some states rely more upon information from neighbors and acquaintances of the recipients than on home visitation. Of course, the accuracy of these persons' statements may sometimes be suspect, but with these and documentation of income by the recipient, the agency will probably have as accurate a picture of the home situation as if the caseworker had made a visit.

4

LEGAL ISSUES OF ADMINISTERING
PUBLIC ASSISTANCE

With the creation of the Interstate Commerce Commission in 1887, independent administrative agencies became an integral part of the governmental operations of the United States. The need for other executive agencies has since become clear; neither Congress nor the courts are in a position to assume the details of rulemaking or the composition of continuous policy statements; neither are either of these major branches in a position to administer "preventive legislation" in the form of licensing or inspections. Executive agencies are expected to develop expertise and expeditiousness within their functions to a level that is wholly unfeasible for the legislature or judiciary.

Yet the administrative agencies themselves have grown so large in terms of personnel alone that they are certainly not as monolithic in character as some citizens might imagine. The three major operations of the agencies — investigation, rulemaking, and adjudication — are themselves complex functions in which no single person can develop total competence. Agency decision making is concerned with a number of diverse fields, principally the imposition of sanctions; ratemaking, licensing, and other regulatory issues; environmental and safety matters; awards of benefits, loans, grants, and subsidies; inspections, audits, and approvals; and planning and general policy making.[1]

In 1939, President Franklin Roosevelt commissioned Attorney General Frank Murphy to prepare a comprehensive report on procedures within the various executive agencies. Murphy's report, which was released in 1941, is now considered a classic work in its field. It emphasized the need for the independence of the adjudicator in the hearing process as well as the significance of "informal" hearings within the whole administrative process. In other words, the report stressed the necessity of viewing the administrative process as an independent legal model. Largely as a result of the Murphy report, Congress began work on the creation of the Administrative Procedure Act (APA), which became a reality in 1946.

The APA has been described as a compromise ". . . between those who opposed any effort to require uniformity and judicalization in the administrative process, on the one hand, and the ABA and allied proponents of procedural reform or curtailment of administrative powers, on the other."[2] The APA was supported by the President and by the American Bar Association (ABA) as it attempted to prevent arbitrary procedural action on the part of agencies so that investigations, rulemaking, and adjudications would assure basic fairness. There is still some faint advocacy within the American Bar Association for more formalization of administrative procedures and the creation of administrative courts that would take the adjudicatory function from agency heads in order to reach a higher level of due process.

Agency power has steadily become more pervasive in daily governmental operations. "Agencies may set rates, deny permission to undertake or drop a service, order reorganization or dissolution of a company, take or limit the use made of one's property, require detailed record keeping and reporting, or issue subpoenas requiring production of information or personal testimony."[3] Because of the flexibility required, especially in the technical areas listed above, and the lack of pertinent data at the lawmaking stage — plus the obstacle of political compromise — Congress can only delegate its general intent to the agencies. The creators of the APA hoped to establish definitive guidelines that would hinder abuse of this "gift."

For three decades, practical use of the Administrative Procedure Act demonstrated that law pertaining to legal procedural concerns must be flexible enough to allow for many interpretations of due process of law. This was well demonstrated in *Mathews* v. *Eldridge.* Therein, the United States Supreme Court *minimized* due process requirements in a Social Security disability hearing by balancing three factors: the interest of the claimant, the risk of erroneous deprivation and probable value of additional due process, and fiscal and administrative burdens. No such balance had been sought in *Goldberg.*

While "administrative procedure should be concerned with the overall fairness and accuracy of decisions, with their efficient and low-cost resolution, and in a democratic society, with participant satisfaction with the process,"[4] agencies need to experiment with these norms of decision making according to the distinctive nature of their own structural-functional organization. For example, fairness, efficiency, and satisfaction will assume different meanings for regulatory agencies than for those dispensing benefits. Determining interstate railroad rates and awarding disability payments are obviously two functions requiring quite different considerations in terms of the human consequences alone.

Because of the diverse interpretations of due process within the administrative realm, some congressional interests proposed revisions of the Administrative Procedure Act.[5] This "new" APA sought to limit trial-type procedures in administrative hearings to the "imposition of a sanction for past conduct" and other cases requiring such treatment under constitutional mandate. The Senate bill also called for a unitary administrative procedure containing "the minimum procedural ingredients of APA informal rulemaking (notice, written comment, and reasons)" and expansion to include oral comment and cross-examination of specific issues determined suitable by the agency.[6]

The vagueness implicit in agency discretion toward cases requiring an adversarial, evidentiary hearing according to constitutional guidelines actually places agency personnel in the role of a federal judiciary, interpreting constitutional provisions. Instead, due process standards in various agency settings should become more clear through explicit legislative statement. Many observers of the federal bureaucracy have had good reason to fear any addition to the pool of administrative discretion.

THE FACT-POLICY DISTINCTION

In establishing the specific due process requirements that must be met by a state "social service" agency before terminating AFDC benefits, the Supreme Court majority in *Goldberg* asserted that these special procedures must be followed in any beneficiary case where "brutal need" and disputed questions of fact are at issue. Even though the Social Security Administration has prided itself on its objective and indeed paternalistic application of policy to real-life situations, any practicing administrative-law judge (ALJ) will undoubtedly question that decisions can be *that* empirically derived. Approximately 90 percent of the cases heard by an ALJ involve a disability claim,[7] and the legal definition of disability is far from exact. Furthermore, different doctors' examinations may give diverse interpretations of the patient's condition. Educational background and work history will also be decisive factors in determining future employ-ability in light of current societal vocational needs.[8]

The impressive 50 percent reversal rate by Social Security ALJs suggests that the application of SSA policy to specific circumstances is not objectively standardized. But can issues of fact and those of policy be consistently distinguished? Can a claimant find satisfaction in questioning the policy by which he or she was treated by the administrative agency as well as questioning the agency's knowledge of the actual facts of the case?

In *Richardson* v. *Wright,* the Court majority refused to rule on the merits of the government's argument that termination of Social Security disability payments without an evidentiary hearing first being held met all due process requirements. The Court justified its indecision by viewing as adequate the Health, Education and Welfare Secretary's recent adoption of regulations providing the beneficiary with notice of the proposed termina-tion and an opportunity to submit a written response.[9] Justice Brennan, joined by Justices Douglas and Marshall, were in dissent against the major-ity of four. Justice Brennan, who wrote the minority opinion, pointed to what he considered to be basic deficiencies in the new HEW regulations, such as no allowance for an evidentiary hearing with oral evidence and cross-examination, no chance for claimant review of the government's file, and no guarantee of a decision by an impartial individual.

Justice Brennan noted that HEW had attempted to differentiate welfare and old-age benefit termination from disability by alleging that the basis of the former was less reliable than the employer wage reports and the medical reports that determined eligibility to disability checks. In rejecting the notion that disability claimants were in less need of an evi-dentiary hearing than welfare beneficiaries, Brennan, who had written the majority opinion in *Goldberg,* stated that in that previous decision the Court had discarded considerations "where there are no factual issues in dispute or where the application of the rule of law is not intertwined with factual issues." In other words, Brennan believed that the *Goldberg* majority had buried the fact-policy distinction forever as having no practi-cal use in judicial reasoning.

To Justice Brennan, the *Richardson* v. *Wright* case should also dis-regard the issue since the determination of disability requires ". . . the resolution of factual issues and the application of legal rules to the facts found." Such a determination demands a hearing because a written presentation by a relatively uneducated claimant without benefit of the flexibility of an oral presentation in any open forum may not offer a fair depiction of the claimant's position. Brennan noted that in *Greene* v. *McElroy,* the Court had ruled that when facts are at issue, cross-examination and review of the government's file will protect any individual against misinformation or malice.

In the following year, *Yee-Litt* v. *Richardson* dispelled much of the confusion about the fact-policy distinction. Herein the California regulations that permitted the reduction or termination of welfare benefits without a prior hearing were challenged on constitutional grounds. The state rules allowed the hearing referee to refuse a hearing if the case raised only an issue of policy as opposed to an issue of judgment of fact. Recipients were not "burdened" with the responsibility of arguing facts if county welfare workers supplied the "necessary" data.

The district court had found the fact-policy distinction exercised by the referee to be too imprecise to justify the termination of welfare aid without a prior hearing. The court, in labeling the distinction as "unclear and unmanageable," did not invalidate it absolutely but was highly critical. The Supreme Court summarily affirmed. Consequently, a state agency may no longer discontinue benefits prior to a hearing based upon the unilateral decision that the claimant's arguments are based solely in matters of policy and not of fact.

Neither "fact" nor "policy" has ever been judicially defined, although Justice Rehnquist in *United States* v. *Florida East Coast Railway* made a distinction between rule-making and adjudication according to the number of people affected by either administrative action. However, one is made to wonder ". . . how the interests of the recipient or the state would change because the recipient attacked the legal basis for his termination rather than the factual basis."[10] In the final analysis, the brutal need of the aged, blind, poor, or disabled will continue, no matter what type of claim is made.

NOTICE AND THE RIGHT TO BE HEARD

Inherent within the relationship between a private individual and an administrative agency about to take adverse action against the individual is the right of that individual to have prior notice and to present his or her case. With the passage of the Administrative Procedure Act in 1946, the administrative sector became more responsive to considerations of basic fairness by providing impartial, agency-independent adjudicators, and a public-hearing forum in a receptive atmosphere, following an orderly and dignified procedural process. Specifically, the APA provided in Section 554 (b) that persons are entitled to timely notice of an impending formal agency hearing regarding their eligibility status, including information concerning "the matters of fact and law asserted. . . . " Sections 556 (c) and (d) assert a private party's right in a formal hearing to present his or her "case or defense by oral or documentary evidence, to submit rebuttal evidence, and to conduct such cross-examination as may be required for a full and true disclosure of the facts."

The Uniform Law Commissioners' Revised Model State Administrative Procedure Act[11] has similar statements regarding notice and the right to be heard. Notice should include "a short and plain statement of the matters asserted" (Sec. 9:b). Of the right to be heard, the act allows that "[o]pportunity shall be afforded all parties to respond and present evidence and argument on all issues involved" (Sec. 9:c).

Associate Justice Felix Frankfurter, in a concurring opinion in *Joint Anti-Fascist Refugee Committee* v. *McGrath,* vividly expressed the significance of the individual's right to be heard before an administrative tribunal. He stated that essential to due process of law is "the right to be heard before being condemned to suffer grievous loss of any kind, even though it may not involve the stigma and hardships of a criminal conviction." Justice Frankfurter continued that "no better instrument has been devised for arriving at truth than to give a person in jeopardy of serious loss notice of the case against him and opportunity to meet it. Nor has a better way been found for generating the feeling, so important to a popular government, that justice has been done." The justice's second comment pungently points to the two most positive characteristics of an open-hearing forum—namely, accuracy ("arriving at the truth") and legitimacy ("feeling . . . that justice has been done").

The hearing environment presents a chance for accurate discovery by presentation of evidence; the sense of legitimacy may bring voluntary compliance and possibly a negotiated settlement.[12] Thus, it can be implied that inherently founded within the concept of due process of law are the pragmatic considerations of a hearing providing the best setting in which an accurate depiction of the facts can be obtained,[13] as well as convincing the citizenry that the procedures to which they are subject are legitimate. With these justifications, as well as the cornerstone of government-protected inalienable rights, the evidentiary hearing has assumed a central position in the administrative process.

THE RULES OF EVIDENCE

The "tone" for the rules of evidence followed within the administrative context was first set forth, as has been already mentioned, in Attorney General Frank Murphy's report to President Franklin Roosevelt. Therein it was specified that because of the use of a hearing officer rather than a jury and the technical matters considered, formal rules of evidence would act against the flexibility intended for administrative procedures. Also, and most importantly, an agency adjudication must decide both the particular case at hand and how that decision will affect the whole public interest. Consequently, according to the report, *all* evidence should be admissible which is "reliable, probative and relevant." Only a significant ". . . probability of error justifies the burden of stricter methods of proof."[14]

The 1946 Administrative Procedure Act captured the spirit of Murphy's report by providing that the burden of proof must rest with the agency, "the moving party" under common law, unless otherwise specified by statute. The agency must therefore be receptive to all oral or documentary evidence that is not "irrelevant, immaterial, or unduly repetitious." The record is to be supported by "reliable, probative and substantial evidence." Unless a piece of evidence falls under one of the three forbidden categories above, the claimant has the right to present any points of fact to aid his or her case.[15]

In studies of disability claims, it has been demonstrated that medical evidence submitted by the beneficiary with the help of an attorney and buttressed by expert witnesses enhances the chance of the claimant to receive a favorable decision to obtain or continue benefits of up to 91.1 percent.[16] Furthermore, during the period of preparation for the case, the government must make its files available to the claimant so that he or she may fully understand the issues involved.[17] This specific provision is part of the HEW regulations adopted directly after the *Goldberg* decision.

Written Evidence

Written evidence, as opposed to oral testimony, is considered peculiarly appropriate to the administrative process. The 1941 report of Attorney General Murphy specified that a case might well be reduced "to verified written statements which are exchanged by the parties for purposes of rebuttal; the case is then decided upon the papers thus submitted."[18] Such a "written" hearing is especially appropriate in cases involved with technical matters or those based on written records. Only for needed clarification would the author(s) of such writings be called to give oral testimony and possibly to face cross-examination. Section 556(d) of the Administrative Procedure Act states that as long as a party will not be prejudiced, all or part of the evidence received in a hearing may be presented in written form. The Model State Administrative Procedure Act follows suit in its Section 10 by allowing that ". . . when a hearing will be expedited and the interests of the parties will not be prejudiced substantially, any part of the evidence may be received in written form."

Virtually all the "beneficent" agencies as well as the Interstate Commerce Commission, the Department of Agriculture, and the National Railroad Adjustment Board have used written testimony extensively, as in rate and price control cases. Written evidence is especially useful to administrative agencies dispensing benefits that are simply attempting to ascertain the eligibility of claimants for benefits; these are not considered adversarial proceedings in which the government and the individual are positioned on opposing sides. Agencies that deal in numerous, relatively small claims are also prone to accept only written evidence, since additional administrative costs might be difficult to justify. Once provision has been met for written statements to be exchanged by the parties to allow for rebuttal, the APA requirements have probably been met.[19]

Several factors inherent in administrative proceedings make written evidence suitable to them. First, it is assumed that an administrative judge of facts can more ably discern reliable from unreliable evidence than can a jury. Second, agencies are more likely to be concerned with general possibilities than with the question of a given individual's guilt. Third, most administrative proceedings are subject to the need for more rapid decision making in the realm of probative value as opposed to judicial "truth." Also, "demeanor evidence" offered by the personal appearance of witnesses — oftentimes government employees — is not as determinate a variable as it might be in a jury trial. Fourth and last, "hearing" by administrative investigation, and its consequent report, may be more meaningful to an agency than an initial formal hearing.[20] If there are substantive questions as to how the agency reached its decision, then a structural hearing can be made available.

There is much to value in the use of written evidence by administrative decision makers. One authority in the field has expressed this idea as follows:

The reduction of expense and delay, the increased availability to the agency of all pertinent viewpoints and material, and the promise of added clarification and precision, all contribute to the conclusion that administrative experimentation with the substitution of written for oral evidence is desirable.[21]

As long as the opportunity for rebuttal is afforded, written evidence can expedite fair administrative proceedings.

Official Notice

Growing from a faith in the cumulative expertise of years of administration is the legal allowance for "official notice." This is analogous to the judicial practice of "judicial notice" in which the judge relies on extra-record information; namely, his legal expertise in reading law and applying appropriate decisions already rendered to the case at hand. "Judicial notice," however, must be more limited in scope than "official notice" because there is less opportunity for rebuttal of disputed facts in a courtroom than in an agency hearing, which offers notice and rebuttal and allows for any party in the hearing to suggest "official notice" to certain facts.

Agencies have found the use of official notice acceptable to the courts, especially when used in conjunction with technical matters that may well have become somewhat common knowledge among persons working in a defined administrative field over a period of time. Certainly administrative-law judges are not expected to forget all the knowledge that they have accumulated over years of hearing cases in such an area as disability which demands some level of medical expertise. "Official notice is concerned with the *process of proof,* not with the *evaluation of evidence.*" Indeed, "the difference between an administrative tribunal's use of nonrecord information included in its expert knowledge, as a substitute for evidence or notice, and its application of its background in evaluating and drawing conclusions from the evidence that is in the record, is primarily a difference of degree rather than of kind."[22] Thus, the examiner is placed in the role of evaluating "proof" as opposed to evaluating evidence.

The Administrative Procedure Act (APA) provides in Section 556(c) that if an agency decision rests upon any "material fact" of which official notice is taken, a party is entitled to an opportunity to refute that evidence. The Model State APA (Sec. 10:3) is more specific in requiring open acknowledgment of facts taken by official notice even to "staff memoranda or data," but surely recognizes the value of an agency's expertise in evaluating evidence. Official notice meets due process requirements as long as a chance for rebuttal is afforded and the subject is appropriate for notice.

There is, of course, some subject matter not appropriate for judicial — official — notice. Certainly the disputed facts of the particular case at hand should not be treated in this way nor should any legal standards used in the judgment. The testimony of expert witnesses may, however, be given official notice so that the claimant's attorney may have an opportunity to refute the evidence such persons offer. In *Perales,* expert testimony was held to be admissible as long as it was relevant to the inquiry at hand. Some studies on the other hand indicate that vocational experts, in particular, do not necessarily enhance the claimant's chances for success in a nonadversarial hearing.[23]

Hearsay

The rules of evidence under administrative law are much less stringent than those found within courtroom walls. This situation is largely permissible because administrators are considered to be more discerning judges of the reliability of evidence than juries. In fact, in the administrative realm, the "competency of evidence is not the same thing as credibility of evidence. Evidence may be incompetent yet credible."[24] The Model State APA (Sec. 10:1) specifically allows for the admission of any evidence that ". . . is of a type commonly relied upon by reasonably prudent men in the conduct of their affairs." Any objections to such evidence must be noted in the record.

The hearsay rule, when used even in the courtroom is marked by so many exceptions[25] that the observer will probably become convinced that the *reliability* of the evidence seems to be the most controlling consideration. The federal APA (Sec. 556:d) allows the introduction of "any oral or documentary evidence" which is supported by other "reliable, probative, and substantial evidence." In *Perales,* hearsay was held admissible as *part* of the evidence as long as it had probative value for the hearing. Hearsay, however, must be backed by substantial evidence, meaning that the decision must be supported by some evidence that is subject to cross-examination.[26] Of course, some evidence considered *substantial* lacks a *high* level of corroboration, and so the ". . . kind of evidence on which responsible persons are accustomed to rely in serious affairs" (i.e., hearsay)[27] may prove to hold considerable weight in an administrative hearing.

Professor Ernest Gellhorn offers several elements in evaluating the worth of hearsay: What facts are offered by the evidence? Is there better evidence available? Could the cost of acquiring "better" evidence be justified? What level of precision should the agency's fact-finding demand? Does administrative policy behind the agency's enacting statute justify a high level of diligence in adjudicatory discovery?[28] All these considerations will obviously color the agency's decision to admit certain points of hearsay evidence as long as the hearsay appears to be credible.

RIGHT TO COUNSEL AND CROSS-EXAMINATION

The right to legal counsel and the often-accompanying right to cross-examination of adverse witnesses has long been an intricate aspect of Sixth Amendment criminal-trial protections. The federal (Sec. 556:c) and Model State (Sec. 9) Administrative Procedure Acts do not *demand* the presence of attorneys in formal administrative hearings but do provide the hearing examiner(s) with enough control of the hearing proceedings to assure the fair presentation of both sides of the issue at hand — that is, if the hearing officer is willing to assume the burden implied. Both acts also make provision for presentation of a defense against the agency's case. The federal APA states:

. . . A party is entitled to present his case or defense by oral or documentary evidence, to submit rebuttal evidence, and to conduct such cross-examination as may be required for a full and true disclosure of the facts.[5 U.S.C.A., Sec. 556:d]

The Model State APA (Sec. 10:1,2) specifies that objections to any evidence offered will be accepted and noted in the record and that a party may conduct cross-examination to reach an accurate picture of the facts.

After the *Goldberg* decision, the United States Department of Health, Education and Welfare adopted regulations providing the claimant's right to representation by counsel or a friend and the right to challenge any evidence or testimony.[29] The 1973 HEW regulations, however, placed no obligation upon the agency to inform a claimant of ways in which to obtain legal counsel for his or her hearing, as had been the case previously.[30] Hence, a claimant may not use the option of having legal representation because of sheer ignorance about its existence, and yet the right to counsel is often inherent in the most basic "right to be heard." It is important, however, to remember that an attorney will not always be the best representative. Indeed, when appearing before the Internal Revenue Service, one's accountant might well prove to be of considerably more use. The issue is obviously one of *appropriate* representation.

In most cases, a claimant's interests are more certain to be protected if he or she has legal counsel. It is tenuous at best in many cases to rely upon one hearing officer to see that the arguments for both the claimant and the agency are revealed as well as weighing those arguments to reach a decision. The Supreme Court seemed to recognize this need in 1973, in *Gagnon* v. *Scarpelli,* when it ruled that in probation and parole hearings where an indigent person is unable to represent himself or herself, to handle documentation or cross-examination, or where criminal prosecution seems possible, an attorney should be assigned. This rule could be used on a case-by-case basis, leaving the appointment of legal counsel to the discretion of the hearing examiner. Could most persons, however, whether indigent or not, fully represent themselves in an evidentiary hearing and fully judge the importance of that role?

The significance of legal representation is even more clearly illustrated by the possibility of welfare investigations themselves becoming incriminatory of the claimant. Even though one state supreme court in *State* v. *Graves* held that the questioning of a welfare claimant which could lead to conviction for fraud is permissible "as long as it is not threatening or overbearing and the individual is free to leave," there is some question as to how "free" any claimant of benefits on which he or she is dependent for sustenance is going to feel when responding to questions of the agency representative. The court therein held that because the claimant was unaware of state regulations that would have threatened the loss of her benefits for noncooperation, she was not coerced, but there is little doubt that she might well have intuitively concluded what her fate might be for not answering agency inquiries. At least, one might conclude from this decision that *Miranda*-like warnings should be applied in situations where the claimant is plainly unaware of such regulations. As in any other occasion of a person's being questioned by the state, the individual's right against self-incrimination is best sheltered by the presence of competent legal counsel.

One relatively recent study of legal representation in nonadversary (disability) hearings emphasized the multisided role which attorneys may play in such proceedings.[31] The study showed that at the Social Security hearing stage, a claimant's chances of winning on the issue of his or her wage-earning capacity were significantly improved in 86 percent of the cases if an attorney was present. In these same cases, the data showed that the testimony of expert witnesses was not an adequate substitute for legal representation.

Besides enhancing the opportunity for success, the legal representation of a claimant fosters faith in the fairness of the hearing process; the claimant is more likely to believe that his or her contribution to a hearing following procedural due process guidelines has had a bearing on the decision rendered. If legitimacy is as important a consideration as accuracy in assessing the administrative hearing process, then a claimant is much more likely to believe he or she has had the opportunity fully to exercise his or her "right to be heard" through legal representation. Consequently, agencies should at least inform a claimant of sources of legal counsel, if they are not willing to provide the service automatically.

Allied to the right to skilled representation is the right of cross-examination of the agency's adverse witnesses. Questioning of adverse testimony, although it may serve to review the intricacies of statements made and to assess the "demeanor" of the witnesses,[32] is not considered to be absolutely necessary in all administrative proceedings. In fact, it is usually a matter left to the discretion of the hearing examiner as to whether cross-examination will enhance the fact-finding expedition of the hearing. Only with the *Goldberg* requirements was cross-examination demanded in Social Security welfare hearings, and even then, it might not be fully realized without legal counsel.

It is true that on occasion written evidence may well substitute for oral testimony in administrative hearings because the case may require only the application of fairly objective agency policy to a fact-situation. Yet the burden of judgment upon the hearing examiner is awesome, and in doubtful cases the hearing officer would be prudent to allow for cross-examination. There is no better way to test accuracy, "probe truthfulness," "question memory and narration, and to expose the bias of any opinion. . . ."[33] If a sufficient opportunity for rebuttal is allowed, however, the urgency for cross-examination may be reduced, which was the Court's reasoning in *Perales* where the omission of cross-examination of those doctors submitting written medical diagnoses was not held to be unfair.

AN IMPARTIAL DECISION MAKER

An impartial decision maker as an intrinsic part of the administrative hearing process was highly recommended in Attorney General Murphy's 1941 report. Therein, the President was advised to establish within the agencies a group of designated, salaried hearing officers who would preside over the disposition of cases and who would be uninvolved in the prosecutory and investigative functions of the agency. Following suit, the federal APA (5 U.S.C.A., Sec. 554:c) demanded a strict separation of function to ensure impartiality while the Model State APA (Sec. 13) provided that an agency decision maker can conduct ex parte consultations with other agency members as long as official notice is taken of the action. The regulations of the Department of Health, Education and Welfare after the *Goldberg* decision also placed strictures against bias by specifying that no person making the decision of denial at the local level should have a part in the final administrative determination.[34]

The writers of the Federal Administrative Procedure Act rejected the idea of having a totally separate corps of hearing examiners apart from the agencies. Effective administrative expertise among the adjudicators was thought to be more feasible if the judges were part of agency personnel. Surely one could hold to agency policy and still be unbiased in a particular case. This was considered quite an improvement over the period prior to 1946, when an agency could choose anyone to be a hearing examiner, and usually the choice hinged upon the degree of a candidate's ineptness. Oftentimes, hearing decisions were actually written by agency attorneys, even before the hearing had come to a close.[35] Of course, the most recent revolution in the status of federal hearing officers occurred in 1972, when "examiners" became "administrative law judges,"[36] finally achieving real judicial status.

Personal and/or institutional bias is one of the three points considered during any judicial review of agency action. A court will accordingly consider the procedures followed, the appropriateness of standards, and the sufficiency of evidence. If a court can see any personal bias other than that of expertise or prejudgment of the rightness of legislative policy, the hearing decision will fall. Institutional bias may be seen in the informality of an actual adversary setting, the level of discretion left to expert decision makers, and the decision maker's relationship with other agency members. In supplying due process procedures to shelter the claimant from agency bias, the Court may well have been establishing standards for agency action against which judicial review can become more systematized.[37]

The "separation of function" issue has been the target of much attention for it is obviously at this point that the average claimant, especially one without a legal representative, is likely to feel the agency has merely appointed a hearing officer to support its side of the controversy. It is difficult for the layman to appreciate the differences between a judicial and administrative setting and that the hearing officer may actually be a "finder of fact" as well as adjudicator in order to expedite the proceedings. Of course, there must be supporting evidence to the hearing officer's investigative findings but his or her impartiality in maintaining the integrity of agency policy is assumed.

A hearing officer must be open to the submittal of new evidence which can persuade him or her to a change of thinking. It is not a matter of being indifferent to policy, but rather of just being open to new evidence and of having no personal advantage to gain in the decision rendered. A decision maker must be able to use his or her prior experience and learning. Only should facts and issues involving the same parties reoccur need disqualification be the rule. "Disqualification of judges – and of administrators – does not come to pass because one knows that the hearing *will* be unfair, but because it *might* be unfair."[38]

In *Richardson* v. *Perales,* the Supreme Court substantiated the three-hat role of many administrative-law judges – as in the Social Security Administration – where the judge acts as fact finder for the government and the claimant as well as decision maker. The Court saw no violation of due process in this practice, especially considering the nearly 50 percent reversal rate of ALJs over state disability denials. Some observers, however, see the responsibility laid on hearing officers as too great a burden so that the government, like the claimant, should have representation in an administrative hearing, even if both parties merely use paralegal representatives. Yet this will not answer the issue of the fact finder developing a narrowly channeled expertise in inquiry that may fashion the decisions he or she makes into products of rigid formula. Most administrative adjudicators typically hear cases that fall within rather confined subject areas. Although the expertise they develop aids in efficient decision making, this specialization may interfere with the usage of other important characteristics in these officers, such as "impartiality," "objectivity," and "independence." One jurist pointed to this obstacle by stating that "one of the dangers of extraordinary experience is that those who have it may fall into the grooves created by their own expertness."[39] Expert fact finders may find their preconceptions prohibitive to an honest weighing of the facts in a given situation. Also, special agency qualifications for ALJs within the selective certification process of the Civil Service Commission give agency attorneys a favored position toward receiving an ALJ appointment. These persons may not bring as comprehensive a perspective to the ALJ role as would be desirable.

Fear arises when outsiders who are the heads of agencies become involved in preliminary decisions or in checking hearing officers' decisions, the feeling being that the decision maker's loyalty to agency subordinates may color his or her decision, as will their ex parte consultations with him. A hearing officer, however, can certainly benefit from the expert knowledge of the administrators with whom he works. If functions were totally segregated in an agency's operations, there would be fewer informal conciliations of adversaries and more litigation. Within a system of overlapping functions — as long as bias is not evident — it is easier to determine if a case actually exists between two parties.[40] It also is important to remember that agencies are organizations consisting of many persons as is the state that stands behind them. Consequently, there will be no single strain of opinion on any given issue, and no agency will act as a single-minded Leviathan against the interests of the individual citizen.

THE RECORD AND JUDICIAL REVIEW

The federal APA (5 U.S.C.A., Sec. 557:c) assured that every decision in an adjudicatory proceeding would produce "a statement of findings and conclusions, and the reasons or basis therefore, on all material issues of fact, law, or discretion presented on the record." The findings of fact should demonstrate that the administrative decision came from the evidence and the law rather than from extraneous considerations of the hearing examiner. The evidence should be examined as to its "accuracy and credibility"; the evidence, if vital, will then lead to a determination of facts within the general context of the law and the agency's enacting statute, in particular.[41]

The Model State APA (Sec. 9:g) followed a similar rationale by stating that "findings of fact shall be based exclusively on the evidence and on matters officially noticed." Also, "a final decision shall include findings of fact and conclusions of law, separately stated" (Sec. 12). HEW regulations following the *Goldberg* decision also enforced the requirement of a decision based on the record, which is limited to the evidence presented at the hearing. State fair hearings were required to specify the evidence backing the reasons for the decision.[42] These regulations were reinforced by the Disability Insurance Amendments of 1979 which provided that "notice to claimants for benefits will provide a brief statement of the pertinent law and regulations, a concise summary of the evidence and reason for the decision."[43]

The findings of fact of an administrative decision serve several substantial purposes. They demonstrate the care taken in developing the decision so that the parties involved will feel themselves justly treated. Carefully formulated decisions encourage the agency to build a body of case "law" from which precedents can be drawn. Finally, the hearing record, including the findings of fact, serves as the basis for possible judicial review.

In 1902, the United States Supreme Court launched the presumption of the reviewability of agency action by the courts. In *American School of Magnetic Healing* v. *McAnnulty*, the Post Office Department had stopped the mailing of an electrical device claimed to have healing capacities on the basis of alleged fraud. The Court held that there must be judicial review for such agency action whether or not the U.S. Post Office was correct in its judgment. In fact, the Court noted, electricity was so new that no one at that time could fully realize its potentialities. Two relatively recent Court decisions have confirmed judicial review of agency decision making.[44]

The Federal APA (Sec. 706) is reasonably explicit in defining the scope of judicial review of agency action, although deciding under *one* point of review whether agency action has been "arbitrary, capricious, an abuse of discretion, or otherwise not in accordance with law" may require much judgment. In contrast, most state agencies lack ample statutory guidance for their actions, so that the courts may have to be especially conscientious in reviewing citizen complaints against state administrative agencies. Professor Frederick Davis asserts that such reviews are likely to consider (1) the nature of the interests, i.e., liberty or property; (2) the selectivity of the action — the more selective the government action, the more likely a constitutional requirement exists; (3) administrative costs; (4) the directness of the government action in affecting potential complaints; (5) the stigma effect of the action; and (6) the rule under which the agency is operating.[45]

Davis emphasizes that the courts are attempting to abandon the somewhat vague standards of "arbitrary, capricious, or an abuse of discretion" in any review of nontrial procedures. Rather, the courts will scrutinize how the agency supported its decision and, in so doing, determine whether it failed to comply with a procedure required by law or regulation, misconstrued a statute, exceeded its delegated power, or ignored informal precedent. The consistency and standardization inherent in these suggested changes in review policies would seem to be desirable in both formal and informal agency hearings. Certainly the possibility of the development of a body of precedent in administrative law is intriguing although this would require the publishing of all agency decisions.

There is no claim that judicial review should become a substitute for agency decisions, but it does serve to

test whether the agency (a) has exceeded its constitutional or statutory authority, (b) has properly interpreted the applicable law, (c) had conducted a fair proceeding, and (d) has not acted capriciously or unreasonably.[46]

The possibility of judicial review is a significant check on arbitrary agency action against the individual.

FAIR PROCEDURE AND THE WELFARE HOME VISIT

No analysis of the legal issues of administrative procedures would be complete without some mention of the search and seizure questions within agency home visitation. Are such "visits" inspections or searches? Must a welfare recipient be forced to sacrifice his or her privacy in order to be the recipient of government benefits?

The Federal APA (5 U.S.C.A., Sec. 555:c,d) views all administrative investigations as aids in meeting the needs of the claimant, but at times the agency may have to face possible prosecution — e.g., for fraud — as a motivation. The act requires that an investigation be authorized by law and conducted for a legitimate purpose; the information sought should be reasonable; and the information sought cannot be demanded if privileged, perhaps incriminating. State laws usually require a warrant upon probable cause and a statement that entry has been sought and refused. In attempting an inspection, an agency is expecting compliance; with a search, there is an implied guilt.[47] *People* v. *Laverne,* a state court precedent, acknowledges this distinction: the court held that the violation of an inspection should not automatically result in a penalty; the individual should be given an opportunity to make amends.

In *Camara,* the Court rejected the supposition that a warrantless search automatically meets the Fourth Amendment reasonableness requirement if it is an administrative, civil inspection rather than a criminal search. In *U.S.* v. *Biswell,* however, the Court ruled that when a person is dealing in a business whose regulation is merited by the public interest, he or she must be willing to submit to periodic inspection. Such a "reasonable" inspection does not seem to require a warrant under the Fourth Amendment.

Is such public interest demonstrated in the visit by a caseworker to the home of a welfare recipient? In *Wyman,* the Court saw such a public interest, whether the agency was motivated by a routine contact or a suspicion of fraud. Taxpayers have the right to know how their money is being spent even to the point of forcing a claimant to surrender his or her privacy. Thus, consent to a search — no matter how unreasonable — may be coerced by the need for benefits. Further, a claimant may be faced with criminal prosecution for misrepresentation of eligibility.

In order to be reasonable, even a warrantless search should be backed by some standardized scheme of probable cause and the belief that such a visit will be helpful to the claimant or agency administration of benefits. Such vague "justifications" for home visits as protecting the children or offering nebulous rehabilitation through such visits simply lack rational backing. Why should the welfare home be considered more likely to permit child abuse? How will a home visit by a caseworker "rehabilitate" the claimant? Why should rehabilitation even be an administrative goal? Is it not likely that most welfare claimants would very happily escape from their circumstances, if only it were possible?

In conclusion, this chapter has reviewed the major issues of administrative law revolving around the administration of public assistance. The atmosphere of the administrative hearing is obviously designed to offer an open forum for claimant participation. This paternalistic, non-adversarial setting, however, may serve only to place the claimant in a dependent role rather than assess fairly his or her claim in the light of agency policy.

5

ADMINISTRATIVE
ORGANIZATION AND MOTIVATION

The formalized hearing is a method of getting at the truth and of assuring justice; but it is only one of many methods. No particular means is invariably synonymous with the fair result. No one device can properly assert a monopoly over the procedural virtues, and thus debar efforts to build new, perhaps more direct roads to justice.[1]

Professor Walter Gellhorn's statement above well expresses the understanding that no procedural method guarantees absolute fairness; alternative approaches are always available for consideration and should be explored. Although the Social Security Administration has been working under a paternalistic posture ever since its inception, some critics would admonish the agency to become more formalized in its hearing processes and thus, in the minds of some, more adversarial. A relatively recent Supreme Court decision, *Weinberger* v. *Salfi*, has, however, been less critical. Therein, the Court encouraged the Social Security Administration secretary to be flexible in construing the statutes regarding hearing requirements so that efficient administration of the agency might be adequately assessed. Thus, contingent upon sound management techniques, the due process standards for the administrative hearing process should be sufficiently elastic to suit the circumstances of the hearing itself as well as the subject matter considered in the hearing.[2]

In *Goldberg*, the Supreme Court certainly made mighty strides toward standardizing the procedural due process requirements of at least one area of administrative function; namely, welfare administration. The need for the *Goldberg* format was then rather clear. Prior to *Goldberg*, as the dissenters therein noted, the Department of Health, Education and Welfare regulations required that with adverse agency action pending, a claimant should be informed of his or her right to a hearing, the right to an attorney and be given a clear explanation of these rights and possible sources for legal representation. One study, however, showed that only nine states complied with these HEW strictures in dealing with welfare recipients.[3] Furthermore, most states put restrictions upon the request for a hearing and disallowed recipient review of the investigative file. One-half of the states were not concerned with the impartiality of the decision maker, and only one-third of the states required the decision to be based wholly on the record.

Perhaps the most telling indication of state abuse was that *none* of the states had applied for federal funds to subsidize legal-aid attorneys. Effective as of July 1, 1969, HEW regulations required that an attorney be made available for those claimants requesting one to represent them in a public welfare hearing.[4] After *Goldberg,* however, this regulation was repealed, since the Supreme Court only required that a claimant be informed of his right to legal counsel, not that such representation be supplied.

Another indication of the need for more standard procedures in welfare hearings was a study contrasting urban and rural welfare offices within the state of Virginia.[5] This study found that rural welfare departments within Virginia were less sympathetic to the poor than their urban counterparts and were often found in intentional violation of state and federal law in welfare administration. One example of such violation was the refusal to provide Aid to Families of Dependent Children to admittedly illegitimate children. While the need for public assistance might be more severe in rural areas, a lesser amount of aid appeared to be dispensed there. The importance of attempting to train caseworkers to realize that public assistance is designed to relieve human suffering and, in this instance, the suffering of children cannot be overstated.

In 1973, the Department of Health, Education and Welfare issued regulations drastically affecting the administration of AFDC, as well as of Medicaid, throughout the states.[6] By terming welfare benefits "assistance" rather than "entitlement,"[7] the new regulations hinted of an alteration in HEW's attitude toward the right to receive payments. It was with these regulations that state agencies became no longer required to provide information on how to obtain an attorney for an upcoming hearing.[8] In order for a claimant to request a hearing, he or she must now submit a written request,[9] which for many welfare recipients would pose a major obstacle to being heard. Other 1973 regulation changes include timely notice being reduced to only ten days[10] and recoupment of benefits possible from the time the hearing was requested to the denial of benefits in the hearing.[11] Although none of these changes altered the specifications of *Goldberg,* the spirit in which the agency administered the benefits shifted to more responsibility resting on the claimant to assert his or her procedural rights rather than the agency's encouraging him or her to do so. Indeed, *Goldberg* itself only required the procedures outlined therein to be followed when the case presented a balance between fiscal costs and the extremity of starvation for the claimant.

One other vantage from which to assess the need for standardization in the administration of welfare would be the caseworker's perspective of the procedural requirements of *Goldberg.* A rather comprehensive study of this topic was conducted in the early 1970s; the researcher received a 71 percent rate of return on questionnaires coming from forty states.[12] This study demonstrated a general familiarity among caseworkers with state and federal hearing regulations and with the appeals process itself. The majority of the responding caseworkers felt the hearing process to be important but not essential to welfare administration, while less than one-half expressed the importance of their giving recipients a full explanation of the hearing process. Their hesitancy to explain the process was apparently not the result of institutional pressure, however, but rather of their individual attitudes. Furthermore, 42 percent of those responding were ambivalent as to the need for legal representation in a welfare hearing.

Perhaps the most encompassing inquiry in the study had to do with the caseworker's opinion as to the *right* to public assistance. Overall, the sampling of caseworkers was qualified in its belief in an inherent right to welfare, contending that this right implies the usage of donated privileges, undoubtedly not unlike the attitude of many American citizens. Indeed, "more than two-thirds of the responding sample population expressed attitudes toward the specific factors which in combination resulted in an ambivalent attitude toward the hearing process in general."

Besides assessing the range of attitudes in these caseworkers, the study also produced a perception scale in terms of how the caseworkers perceived their relationship with their clients. It was assumed ". . . that if the workers are found to perceive their relationship paternalistically, the tendency will be greater to impress their views of the hearing process on recipients." This was indeed the perception of 62 percent of the respondents, implying a need to direct and control client attitudes. Thus, while the majority of caseworkers would probably not be antagonistic to the hearing process, they are likely to impart an attitude to their clients of less than full support for a formal hearing. Also, the fact that by encouraging a client to appeal, the caseworker is endangering his or her initial decision means that the caseworker is put in a "Catch-22" position. Obviously, a pattern of reversals on the caseworker's decision is going to place him or her in question with his or her superiors, just as a hearing officer may be questioned for the percentage of reversals within his or her sum total of decisions.

THE QUESTION OF INDEPENDENCE

In the spring of 1979, Congress was faced with a proposal to fix the length of the term of office for federal administrative-law judges (ALJs), at the end of which the appropriate agency would recommend to the Administrative Conference[13] whether a judge should or should not be retained.[14] Thus, ALJs would supposedly become more responsible to the particular agencies they served. Indeed, one ALJ told this writer that, during times of low funds in the Social Security Administration pool, indirect agency pressure had been exerted on ALJs, including himself, to reverse fewer state denials of benefits. Apparently, independent judgment has already been in danger upon occasion in the SSA. Somewhat ironically, one point especially emphasized by Attorney General Murphy's historic report to President Roosevelt was that formal administrative hearings would necessarily require independent adjudicators.

The Social Security Administration Office of Hearings and Appeals (OHA) is probably the largest adjudicative agency in the Western world with more than 625 ALJs who disposed of 180,000 cases in fiscal 1976.[15] In comparison, the federal district courts, courts of appeals, and the Supreme Court have a composite total of 505 judges who terminated 129,683 cases in 1976. These statistics alone justify an emphasis on the SSA as indicative of the federal administrative-hearing process. That about 90 percent of the SSA hearings are under Title II (disability) and Title XVI (supplemental security income) further supports study of the SSA hearing process since it encompasses such a large portion of federal administrative hearings.

The Social Security Administration interpets its relationship with beneficiaries even at the hearing stage as "friendly," but this does not mean that ALJs are thus subject to less stringent review than more adversarial judges. Also, the fact that ALJs are likely to be former employees of the agency they serve because various federal agencies have emphasized appropriate regulatory experience in selecting ALJs[16] does not necessarily harm the quality of review. The historical context from which ALJs are now reviewed sets the tone for present-day policies. The earliest examples of administrative hearing officers were subordinate employees — usually not attorneys — of the agencies themselves who would decide upon such factors as the admissibility of evidence, the credibility of testimony, and the need for a transcript of the proceedings.[17] These persons might have been involved in the initial agency decision and yet were expected to monitor the hearing stage and then submit the record to the agency heads for final determination. In 1917, the Interstate Commerce Commission began a procedural tradition, still followed in federal administrative agencies, whereby hearing officers submitted their own analysis of the hearing as part of the record. Such a report, however, has no defining influence on the agency head.

The agency head makes the final decision for the whole agency. While he or she will certainly consider the hearing officer's input, the agency head may reject it for other reasons than legal error or simply because he or she views the case differently. The agency head may decide on the written record alone, not read the entire record; not express his or her rationale on all points; engage in ex parte consultations — whereas the hearing examiner may not; and may assign his or her staff to write the agency opinion. Of course, the agency head must be able to demonstrate that the agency has based its decision on the evidence presented in the record. This will be ascertained when the agency report is submitted to both parties for rebuttal, prior to the final agency decision being given.

Some administrative observers would contend that the review of an ALJ's decision is an inefficient use of the agency's time. Even though the ALJ is required to base his or her determination on "substantial evidence," the opinion is treated as merely another option for consideration. Why should agency policy makers, most of whom lack legal training, review the decision of the ALJ? That these agency chiefs are much more subject to political pressures than ALJs should also challenge the reliability of their review function. Judge Arthur Gladstone, a former ALJ of the

Federal Communications Commission, contends that administrative policy makers should have only *certiorari* appeal, which is true of the Civil Aeronautics Board and a few state agencies. Thereby, the appellant must show grievous error during the hearing to justify appeal, meaning a prejudicial error. Otherwise, the question arises, Why is the expertise of the ALJ developed by having him or her serve only one agency? And why do persons receive training as ALJs if their decisions are given so little weight?

There has been a considerable amount of advocacy for closing the case file after the ALJ has concluded a hearing so that the Appeals Council,[18] if reviewing the decision, will only consider procedural or prejudicial error. This same suggestion was also made in a Disability Insurance Amendment proposed before the House Ways and Means Committee in April 1979. There is the argument, however, that receipt of evidence should be open through the Appeals Council consideration so that the council may function to establish a higher standard of consistency in agency decisions. On the other hand, the Appeals Council reviews on the average only about 5 percent of ALJ allowances through its own motion, and less than half the losing claimants before ALJs appeal to the council. Thus the Appeals Council, acting alone, cannot be expected to standardize the rationale of agency decisions. Furthermore, decisions of the Appeals Council, even though based on "substantial evidence," are not controlling upon the SSA commissioner. Even though it is a "fundamental tenet of administrative adjudication" that Appeals Council decisions should standardize agency action and limit court review,[19] this process is certainly dependent upon the amount of agreement between the agency director and the council itself.

The way in which the Appeals Council can supplement the quality of the product of agency adjudication is by reviewing ALJ decisions for their consistency with established agency policy, rather than making a judgment of law. This is, in fact, the expected role of the Appeals Council, although it has been the target of some criticism from ALJs in not demonstrating much consistency in its own decisions. Professor Mashaw has suggested that the publication of some Appeals Council decisions might serve to encourage consistency in policy interpretation through individual cases and should have as well an influence on the agency director's decisions. Of course, ALJs themselves receive extensive training and retraining in agency policy, so that their decisions are statements made within the framework of agency rules as well as of law. Also, now that Appeals Council decisions are remanded to ALJs with a written explanation of the council's reasoning, there is a greater chance that more understanding of policy will develop between these two levels of decision making.[20]

State hearing officers generally fall into the same quagmire of review as federal ALJs within the agency setting. Overall, these state officials have no statewide qualifications required of them and may even be agency-appointed employees. Consequently, their opinions are given little credence by the courts in review. California has probably been the most progressive state in certifying its hearing officers through its Office of Administrative Hearings, an office wholly independent of other state agencies. Florida has patterned its hearing system after that of California, with the major exception that if a certified officer is not available, a staff member for an agency other than the one conducting the hearing may preside.[21] Although the independence of agency adjudicators has been a matter of some concern, it has not been officially provided for in most states to date.

The courts have not provided explicit guidelines by which to determine the relationship between a hearing officer and his or her superiors. In 1951, in *Universal Camera Corporation* v. *NLRB,* the National Labor Relations Board was instructed to review the hearing examiner's decision as part of the record in assessing the substantiality of evidence. If, however, the hearing examiner had based his or her decision upon the demeanor of a witness, the Supreme Court later ruled in *FCC* v. *Allentown Broadcasting Corporation* that the agency directors were not compelled to agree with the hearing decision simply because it was founded upon such subtle considerations. Rather, the Court held that the agency heads could differentiate between the "demeanor" question and more substantial evidence and, if finding an inconsistency between them, should make their decision based on the latter. Relatively recently, the Circuit Court of Appeals for the District of Columbia has ruled in *Cinderella Career and Finishing Schools, Inc.,* v. *FTC* that agency heads must base their decisions upon the whole record so that they will be deciding from the same evidence available to the hearing examiner.

The above decisions demonstrate that the judiciary certainly has not held the decisions of hearing officers in reverence but has required basic fairness in agency chiefs' evaluations of such decisions. The administrative-law judge (as of 1972) for all his or her independence in the decisions he or she makes is still subject to the agency he or she serves. Not only are ALJ decisions reviewed by agency policy makers, but the workload assignment is made by the agency according to its assessment of his or

her experience and talents, with the consent of the Supreme Court in
Ramspeck v. Federal Trial Examiners.

Besides attempts to guarantee the independence of administrative
hearing officers, there is the search for a means to standardize their
opinions — as mentioned above with the SSA Appeals Council — and thus
increase their productivity. One Social Security Administration employee
informed this writer that in the spring of 1979, there were between eighty
and ninety thousand cases awaiting hearings in the SSA, but with approximately 650 ALJs producing an average of twenty-seven decisions a month,
this was not considered a backlog.[22] It is, however, assumed by some
agency observers that the establishment of standardized management
procedures will enable the administrative agencies to become much more
efficient in the *number* of cases processed. One commentor, in advocating
the writing of a new Federal Administrative Procedure act, suggested that
one provision of the act should be the conducting of regular "procedural
audits" of the agencies, as well as establishing management techniques to
assess "fair, efficient and satisfactory decision-making."[23] There is, of
course, an obvious dilemma in attempting to establish productivity and
accuracy norms for ALJ decisions and still provide the independence
necessary for fair decisions.

"Positive caseload management"[24] requires

(1) standards and methods of measuring the accuracy, timeliness and
fairness of agency adjudications; (2) the continuous evaluation of agency
adjudications with respect to those standards; and (3) the use of the information gathered in the course of evaluation as a basis for improving
adjudicative performance.[25]

The standard of accuracy alone will obviously require exacting
measures of ALJ decisions both in terms of errors in awards and in denials.
A statistical analysis should demonstrate the likely decision in given circumstances by the "average" ALJ, and then all other decisions should be
checked against this standard for error. Even though ALJs were shown by
one study to be the least costly alternative available for federal agency
decision making,[26] they can be made even less costly by a more efficient
disposal of similar cases. Apparently, such productivity norms are under
development within the National Center for Administrative Justice but,
as of the spiring of 1979, they had not yet been put in written form
based on the data already gathered.[27]

The independence of hearing examiners is obviously a matter of some conjecture with some lawmakers believing that appointment for life gives such officials too much freedom from agency review, whereas other students of the administrative hearing process feel that hearing officers, being "closest" to the evidence, should write the agency's final determination. The states also vary widely on this issue, but most seem to discredit the hearing officer's function by not even requiring basic qualifications for the position. The present writer believes that it is possible to have the hearing decisions reviewed in the light of agency policy without demeaning their determinations. However, the proposal in the Senate requiring the review of ALJs' performance seems laden with potential for abuse because of the lack of specific guidelines upon which to conduct the performance appraisal. If volume of decisions or rate of reversals is used as unconditioned criteria, the position of ALJs will be lessened, and this will reinforce the low status of hearing officers within the states. In such an atmosphere neither the states nor the federal government can expect to attract and keep competent persons in these roles. In order to enhance the skills and independence of the administrative law judge, the creation of a corps of judges or a formal court has been suggested.

A CORPS OR A COURT?

In the name of both efficiency and fairness, there has been some backing for the establishment of an entity in which ALJs would function totally separate from any federal administrative agency. Such proposals have taken the form of an independent corps of ALJs, a panel system of ALJs, or the establishment of a court of administrative appeals. A corps of ALJs would allow the judges to develop expertise in many areas of regulatory and beneficiary administration, making each individual judge more flexible in the types of cases he or she was qualified to hear. The corps would also nullify the selective certification process by which employees of agencies are easily escalated to judgeships. The current proposals for the corps, however, do not specify that once a trial-type hearing is held, the decision should be reviewable only by a judicial court, not by an agency executive.[28] Such a stance would certainly lend more weight and credibility to both federal and state administrative adjudicatory decision makers. On the other hand, the judiciary might find itself delayed with administrative appeals with no intermediary review within the agency. Furthermore, there would be no way in which individual agencies could assure some consistency in the adjudicatory application of agency policy to individual cases.

Another proposal to add more dignity to the role of ALJs has been constructed around the idea of an adjudicatory panel system.[29] It is submitted that such a system would build more confidence, especially in disability determinations, which now demonstrate a radical degree of variance among ALJs. The use of a two-member ALJ panel would also reduce the man-hours expended to decide the merits of any one case, and when the two ALJs disagree, a third ALJ could further reduce the work load of the panel by casting the deciding vote. Dr. Jerry Mashaw's study, in which this proposal appears, advocates the ALJ panel system as possibly being more efficient in terms of time, fiscal costs, and consistency of decisions. Mashaw fears that *lay* panels would probably fall short of the last condition of performance. He recommends that the Social Security Administration attempt usage of some ALJ panels — at least, in a laboratory setting. There would undoubtedly be some major administrative problems to resolve in such a panel system. This writer would speculate that disagreements between two-member panels would be frequent — given the lack of definition in disability cases and the asserted independence of ALJs. There is no reason to believe that individual ALJs would work cooperatively with their peers, nor is there any reason to believe that adding a third to the panel will create conditions conducive to a rapid resolution of the case.

The most commonly suggested change in the administrative hearing process is the creation of a new court of administrative appeals. Dr. Mashaw suggests the possibility of such a court to handle, at least, disability cases, the bulk of the SSA hearing load. Such a court would offer the advantages of uniformity in legal principles and decisional outcomes; independence from agency duress; and improved quality of decisions.[30]

Lying at the heart of the controversy over the "court" proposal are the "generalist" and "specialist" positions. Initially, the value of developing expertise in especially technical legal considerations, such as disability, might seem to outweigh the opposite position. There are, however, substantive limitations on the administrative specialist; namely, the ". . . inability to see beyond the narrow confines of his own experience, intolerance of the layman, and excessive zeal in carrying out his own policy regardless of the cost to other, broader interests of society."[31]

Another point regarding a separate court for administrative appeals advocates the value of a judge's being something of a "Renaissance man" in which his eclectic and comprehensive understanding of the whole environment of his particular decision will enable him to look beyond the immediate case to the broad-reaching societal consequences of the alternatives.[32] Such a person can be backed by experts in a particular field but should have a broader context in which to consider the implications of their expertise. Approachability is another factor that, for some observers, makes a specialized court less desirable.[33] If the claimant perceives such a court as less humanistic than a "generalized" district court, the experience of presenting one's claim before such a tribunal may be less than satisfying and engender an ensuing sense of unfairness.

Advocates of the creation of an "administrative court" contend that the adjudicatory process should be taken from agency jurisdiction so that agencies will function only in a rule-making capacity. Certainly administrators who value the development of expertise should favor this separation. The Office of Safety and Health Administration (OSHA) has already initiated this separation of function through an OSHA commission, which while serving as the adjudicatory body for the agency is responsible to the Department of Labor, not the agency itself. The "core" concept is another proposal in which ALJs would develop "cores" of expertise, such as regulation, enforcement, or claims for benefits, rather than more specific specializations, such as taxation, welfare, or disability,[34] pertaining to particular agencies.

Besides the question of the creation of a separate adjudicatory entity in the administrative realm to develop more efficiency, accuracy, consistency, and claimant confidence in the hearing process, greater attention has recently been given to the use of precedent in administrative law. Administrative-law judges do not use the decisions of their peers as precedents nor does the Social Security Administration Bureau of Hearings and Appeal recognize judicial precedent. The same is true of the National Labor Relations Board. The rationale behind this stance is that uniformity of agency policy outweighs external judicial contractions.[35] Uniform adjudicatory positions are, however, not achieved within administrative agencies *because* of the lack of precedent. Of course, a rule of precedent would require agencies to publish those of their hearing decisions that would require a major revision of policy for the Social Security Administration.

Precedent is not an absolute, even in judicial circles, and perhaps not efficiently applicable to administrative agencies. One authority in this field convincingly argues that it would be more effective to establish a standard for injury claims as a remedy for successful claimants in disability proceedings rather than using case precedent.[36] This would be another measure by which administrative decision making could be made more predictable by standardization of the remedies affordable to certain fact-situations.

Central to any effort made toward more standardization in disability determinations is the need to define legal disability. This becomes a highly complex matter when weighing the degree to which an impairment has resulted in activity loss or restriction, the degree to which such an impairment affects normal activities, and the interaction of the claimant's age, education, and prior work experience with his or her functional limitations and how this will affect his or her capacity for work available in the national economy.[37] Administrative-law judges would certainly find their duties easier and perhaps more satisfying with a defined standard for determining those conditions that are indeed disabling.

ADVERSARIAL HEARINGS: EFFICIENT? FAIR?

One of the prominent arguments regarding management issues in due process hearings is the question of whether hearings must be adversarial in order to meet both efficiency and fairness requirements. Some observers argue that an adversarial tension does not exist between an agency and a claimant simply because the latter is complaining about adverse agency action taken against him or her. For instance, a former chief referee of California's Office of Administrative Hearings has stated that "the purpose of the fair hearing is to elicit facts which describe a person's circumstances and then apply those facts in an objective manner to the laws and regulations governing the particular welfare program."[38] In other words, a hearing involves the mere application of administrative policies once the facts are established, a positivist view of the administration of law. Controversy regarding the substance of law and policy occurs once those are written, not in their application.

Throughout the 1970s, there seems to have been increasing uncertainty as to the value of strict, formal procedural hearings when considering the amount of fiscal costs entailed. Overall, the courts have become reluctant to take a hand in allocating public resources, a duty best left to the people's representatives. This is certainly true in cases where the state has argued that funds are simply not available for expenditure, no matter what constitutional issue might be at stake. This principle was expressed succinctly in *Dandridge* v. *Williams* where the Court stated: "The Constitution does not empower this Court to second-guess state officials charged with the difficult responsibility of allocating limited public welfare funds among the myriad of potential recipients." The Court may rest its decisions in cases involving fiscal limitation on different rationale than in other types of cases.

In determining whether an adversarial proceeding will be necessary to meet constitutional requirements, the courts will assess the cost of such proceedings. Evidence now exists that an adversarial setting may increase the time and costs of hearings.[39] Yet there is little doubt that when a beneficiary has been denied government largess, he or she is faced with an adversarial situation in appealing his or her claim beyond the initial agency denial. Whatever the format of procedures used on appeal or whether the agency considers itself a paternalistic protector of claimant rights, the claimant is, nevertheless, contending for approval which has thus far been denied.

An appearance before an agency hearing examiner *does* constitute an adversarial situation. One must work within that context in order to discern the best ways in which to meet such goals as accuracy, accountability, consistency, and claimant satisfaction. An adversarial atmosphere does not necessarily connote formalism in procedure. An adversarial hearing does not inherently exclude some degree of cooperation between the parties in reaching a just solution, does not require a rigid application of standards in administering benefits, and does not exclude agencies from extending more procedural rights than those required by law.[40]

This writer, in observing several disability hearings before Social Security Administration ALJs, was impressed with the lack of formalism in these hearings and yet with the high degree of concern for the claimants demonstrated by the ALJs. In fact, one ALJ indicated that if there should be any doubt in his mind as to the validity of the claimant's case, he would award that person benefits. This same ALJ conducted his own questioning from a standard set of questions he had received while in training with the SSA Bureau of Hearings and Appeals eighteen years previously. In all the hearings that this writer observed, the participants sat around a conference table, and the atmosphere was relaxed. Evidence was casually admitted into the file, copies of most of which the claimant's attorney, if there was one, had already received; claimants without attorneys were themselves allowed to examine the government's file. In one hearing, even a piece of scratch paper on which a now-deceased doctor had prescribed medications for the claimant was admitted as evidence.

The ALJs were quite receptive to the testimony of any suggested witnesses, including close friends and family members of the claimant.

One ALJ stated that he saw no need generally for doctors to testify in disability hearings since they would simply support their written reports. That same ALJ, however, told me of one case in which the doctor had recommended a back operation for a fifty-seven-year-old man, and the ALJ said that he himself had concluded that at that age the man in question could not be helped by a major back operation. He did not discuss any supporting medical evidence for his determination. A doctor's testimony might have changed his general opinion regarding that particular case.

There was certainly no impression given during the observation of these hearings that the hearing officers were advocates for the Social Security Administration and that they themselves were on a campaign to "apprehend" the dregs of society. One of the best examples of this was a previous case in which a physically deformed and mentally borderline claimant had been denied benefits because his record indicated that he had a record of past employment. The ALJ stated that upon reviewing this record, he noticed that the claimant had only been employed by close family members in their own businesses and been assigned to low-responsibility jobs. The judge, therefore, concluded that the likelihood of this person's being hired by anyone outside his family was slight, and awarded him benefits. Obviously in this case, the humanistic considerations determining the decision would not fit every standard mold for all cases in general; it was, however, a just decision.

Basing his decisions sometimes primarily on common sense, this ALJ also presided over a hearing of a twenty-year-old boy who suffered from a severe speech impediment and apparent mental retardation. The ALJ methodically attempted to communicate with the boy and also with the parents. These people were not polished in their presentation, but there was nothing condescending or haughty in the hearing judge's demeanor. He showed a great deal of interest in receiving a fair impression of their homelife with the boy.

Even though the observed ALJs assumed a compassionate attitude toward claimants, they stated a belief that the SSA hearing process is adversarial in nature. They contended that their three-hat role was an unreasonable burden; they advocated the use of claimant and government attorneys in hearings, so that they could act in the role of decision makers alone, rather than having also to develop the facts on both sides of the case. In fact, one ALJ stated that he was sure that if the government had legal representation at his hearings, the percentage of awards to claimants would substantially decrease. Significantly, these judges did not equate the intensification of the adversarial atmosphere of hearings as demanding that they be more formalistic. Indeed, one judge emphasized his apprehension of the clamoring among some ALJs to wear black robes and sit behind benches during the course of administrative hearings.

One area in which hearings can be made more efficient in terms of defining the adversarial issues without infringing upon procedural fairness is by redefining means of discovery.[41] It has been said that ". . . the number of cases which are settled before trial is in direct ratio to the kind of discovery that takes place before trial."[42] Even in Attorney General Murphy's report to President Roosevelt, it was suggested that a prehearing conference to stipulate certain facts of the upcoming hearing could serve ". . . to formulate the issues involved in the hearing, to simplify proof by stipulation, to agree upon the number of witnesses, and to arrange an exchange of exhibits prior to the hearing."[43] By outlining the format of the hearing prior to its occurrence, there would be less contention, and the hearing would operate more expeditiously. Fairness in the prehearing conference would be maintained as long as the right of rebuttal existed.[44]

Administrative-law judges do not now possess the authority to conduct pretrial conferences or to issue subpoenas, to hold persons in contempt, or to administer interrogatories. All these functions serve to provide a hearing with more clearly defined issues, so that human situations can more accurately be assessed by the judge. Ironically, the fact that administrative-law judges do not have these "judicialized" powers tends to slow the process which some would say is already overburdened with formalism.[45]

Certainly in a prehearing, the need for an attorney would seem to be imperative since the structure and content of the hearing are of primary concern to the claimant. While Professor Mashaw's study supports the use of prehearing conferences, subpoenas, and interrogatories, he does not perceive an associated need for legal representation of the claimant. He does, however, contend that the value of counsel is best demonstrated during investigation of the fact-situation as opposed to counsel's role as an advocate during the hearing itself.[46] If an attorney is important as an investigative agent, it seems as if he or she would be indispensable during a prehearing conference when discovery is at issue. Professor Mashaw has, on the other hand, made a strong argument for the complete development of state-level files,[47] which would surely present more verifiable and thus stipulatory material in the prehearing conference.

Social-welfare hearings held at state level are much less structured than those conducted by federal agencies. Because most states lack any substantial statutory guidelines for hearing-officer qualifications, or for hearing procedures, many states "hide behind" the justification of conducting friendly informal hearings, simply because they have no other excuse for the lack of accuracy and consistency in their administrative decision-making processes. In regard to state welfare hearings, one legal authority has contended that "the absence of even general evidentiary standards permits the injection of collateral issues that prolong the hearing, obscure the real issues, and divert the proceeding from the initial task of fact finding."[48] Such circumstances relate directly to the elevated cost and expanded time for the hearing, with no evidence that discovery of the truth of the situation is any more surely guaranteed than in a more efficient process.

In observing several welfare hearings under the auspices of the state of Missouri, this writer sensed a casual atmosphere, with the hearing examiner sitting behind a desk and the claimant and caseworker seated at an adjacent table. The caseworker testified in order to validate agency documentation and to name the regulation, or regulations, under which denial of benefits was required. Hearing examiners for the Family Services Division in Missouri are usually former caseworkers themselves. They are expected to be fact finders during the hearing to assure that the claimant's position was understood — only about 15 percent of the claimants bring attorneys to their hearing, according to one hearing examiner's estimation.

In order to remain impartial in executing his three-hat role, one hearing examiner told this writer that he looked at the file of an upcoming hearing only shortly before entering the hearing room. He also asserted that welfare hearings are rather "cut-and-dried" — in the sense that they involve a simple matter of applying regulations to a set of given circumstances. Hearing examiners in the Family Services Division accept all evidence, since the Missouri APA has no guidelines for hearings. Besides having no procedural guidelines, these hearing examiners are faced with the problem of covering a jurisdiction of many counties — as many at a maximum as thirty. Therefore, much time is spent on the road, which could be used to conduct hearings, in addition to the average twenty-five to thirty cases disposed of in a month.

Substantial suggestions for improving the administrative hearing process have been made by a number of authorities. These proposals revolve around the consideration of adversarial and formalistic aims, which afford a proper balance between individual rights and administrative efficiency. Certainly none of these proposals would advocate that fairness is necessarily sacrificed when procedures become less formal. Professor Frederick Davis expressed this sentiment well, as follows:

Fair procedure is vital even when [the procedure] is entirely as informal as conversation. Informal procedure is not the equivalent of no procedure. For instance, before an agency makes a discretionary determination that affects a party adversely, the procedural protection is very great if the officer will tell the party what he believes the facts to be, and what he contemplates and why, and then if the officer listens to what the party has to say. The fundamentals of procedural fairness can be observed even in an informal conference. . . . [1 Davis, *Administrative Law Treatise* § 4.14 (1965 Supp.)]

Essentially, an open exchange of perceptions of the situation at hand will provide basic fairness.

There has recently been much questioning of the necessity for an adversarial hearing to satisfy due process requirements. Traditionally an adversarial hearing has been thought to have certain advantages, such as providing a neutral terrain on which to be heard, eliciting precise testimony and the opportunity for confrontation in cross-examination. In this way, wrongful deprivation of property may be avoided. But is an adversarial hearing necessary to secure such guarantees? Neutrality may not be offered by a full evidentiary hearing prior to deprivation if the government is forced to continue undeserved benefits throughout the hearing. Other kinds of procedures may offer as high a degree of accuracy as contentious ones. Burdensome administrative costs and unnecessary dependence on adjudication may be caused by the offer of an arena for confrontation in all denial cases.

Because of the above criticisms, it has been suggested that the courts, with the help of adjunct agencies, should become more aggressively investigatory themselves in terms of gathering evidence and formulating relevant issues. A probable-cause finding will result, which will encourage conciliation in most disputes. Up to this point, ". . . neither side would be guaranteed access to the forum and the role of lawyers would be severely restricted." Even if an adversarial trial were requested by the "loser" of the probable-cause finding, great weight would be given to the administrative findings in trial, and the appealing party would have to discredit those findings. Neutrality, accuracy, and confrontation would all be assured under this system, and the problem of claimant passivity would be avoided by using aggressive governmental investigation. Last of all, this reform does not mean abandoning the prior hearing but rather offering this remedy in the most serious disputes and encouraging intra-agency checks on less serious mistakes of agency judgment.[49]

The Florida State Administrative Procedure Act has received some favorable professional comments regarding the distinction it makes between formal and informal hearings.[50] A formal hearing requires a disputed issue of material fact, and both types of hearings require that a "substantial interest" of the claimant has been affected by agency action. The Florida APA is far beyond most state models in providing for a sensible determination of what types of fact-situations require a formal or informal hearing, and also allow the hearing examiner to "re-classify" a hearing in progress as the evidence is developed and lesser or more rigid procedural requirements are needed.

Professor Jerry Mashaw agrees that a trial-type hearing may not be the most appropriate means to protect the rights of a claimant of government benefits. Mashaw argues that even though the United States administrative process is generally presented as being adversarial in content, the context in which neither claimant nor the government is represented by counsel, and the hearing officer merely applies standardized agency rules to particular cases, hardly meets the description. Neither does the evidence indicate that the qualities of fairness, accuracy, and timeliness will be guaranteed in a formal adversarial hearing.

Although quality-control management, when applied in the public welfare sector, has been enforced only to safeguard the public interest from erroneous benefit allocations, Professor Mashaw asserts that it may also help to guarantee a higher degree of fairness, accuracy, and timeliness in welfare administration. Therefore, a formal adversarial hearing process may not be necessary to ensure due process. However, Mashaw warns,

[Moreover], because quality control procedures are directed toward systemic problems rather than the correction of individual errors, the management side of due process can never wholly supplant the need for the more traditional protection afforded by procedural safeguards and appellate review.

Important though for Mashaw is the point that procedural due process does not necessarily require the formalism of *Goldberg*. Rather, the emphasis should be on having "one's claims decided on the basis of all the relevant information," instead of providing each person with an ideal opportunity to participate in the process.

At present, hearings protect claimants only if they themselves are aggressive, informed in welfare law, and can present their case or have access to those who can. Without much doubt, this is simply not generally true of AFDC or disability claimants. As Professor Mashaw emphasizes, an analysis of welfare and disability hearings requires a realistic vantage point from which the available protection for claimant interests must be assessed. "Positive case-load management" makes more sense than an undying faith in the adversarial system, since the latter may simply not fit into the context of crowded case dockets nor the spirit of agency paternalism built into welfare programs. The judiciary will thus be interested in nothing more or less than a showing that the procedures followed, no matter how informal, have supported fairness, accuracy, and timeliness.[51]

For Mashaw, the development of a complete and accurate case file is of more importance in the administrative realm than the contest between adversaries.[52] Mashaw never meets the argument that only the adversarial climate may allow for the full development of "facts" when applied to admittedly complex welfare-agency policies. How can a hearing officer realistically be expected to develop the case file from all angles when he or she is not working in the interest of any one individual or agency? Hearing officers themselves emphasize the impossibility of their assigned task.

HOME VISITATION: TO REDEEM OR TO ACCUSE?

Besides administrative hearings, home visitations by public welfare caseworkers also raise some procedural due process inquiries. As with adversarial hearings, it should be demonstrated that these visits accomplish their stated objectives or the practice will meet neither the requirements of due process nor those of efficient administrative management. One Missouri state welfare supervisor informed this writer that in more than twenty years of experience in welfare casework, she had seldom found home visitation to be of much assistance in determining claimant eligibility. She stated that in only a few instances had she seen a home visit aid the caseworker in better assessing need; one such case involved medical circumstances. She said that once every six months the welfare homes under her office's jurisdiction were visited by appointment, and if the home visit was refused, benefits would in all likelihood be terminated.

More common than home visits in Missouri, however, was the practice of contacting longtime acquaintances of a welfare client to determine whether a father was living in the household as well as declared dependent children. There have been no complaints regarding this practice, according to the caseworker supervisor interviewed.

The *Wyman* decision raised several procedural questions revolving around welfare home visitation, with the Court holding that such visits are not appropriate to the probable cause and warrant requirements of the Fourth Amendment. While in *Goldberg* the Court willingly acknowledged the right to welfare benefits if the recipient was eligible, in *Wyman* the Court seemed to attach a qualification that with the receipt of welfare payments, a person was tacitly implying consent to future home visits by caseworkers. The Court did not address the possibility of a trial for fraud if, based on evidence obtained during a home visit, a state welfare agency charged an individual with misrepresenation or child abuse. Rather, the Court justified the visit or inspection as long as there was no *intent* to discover criminal activity.

The issue of possible criminal prosecution makes the rehabilitative purpose, which is supposedly a motivation in home visits, absurd. How are caseworkers expected to play the schizophrenic role of being both investigators and social saviors? Besides simply not fitting the human condition, with their heavy case loads and constant personnel turnovers, most state welfare agencies cannot absorb the responsibility of trying to rehabilitate welfare recipients back into the societal mainstream. Indeed, the very word "rehabilitate" connotes an undertone of "being in the wrong" and a need to alter that status rather than looking upon welfare recipients as often being the victims of a fluctuating, competitive economic environment that does not equally prepare all citizens to compete successfully.

The suggestion of separating these two roles seems to be cogent.[53] With better-trained caseworkers, attracted by compensatory salaries, the rehabilitative aspect of welfare administration could take on a real meaning in terms of establishing a confidential relationship between the claimant and the caseworker.[54] Such a human connection could be of inestimable value to a claimant trapped by hopelessness, but such confidence will not be engendered if this same caseworker also functions as an agency spy. The latter role must be taken by a separate group of agency employees trained to apply the eligibility formula to particular situations and to investigate suspicions of fraud by visiting the home, armed with a warrant.

The development and possible adjudication of facts should be separated from the implementation of social policy which in itself may be suspicious if the agency attempts to impose its moral values on welfare recipients, such as in the "man-in-the-house" (*King* v. *Smith*) ruling. Therefore, in implementing the intra-agency division of labor, welfare chiefs must realistically accept that caseworkers are ". . . not necessarily ideologically pro- or anticlient but in large part [are] self-interested brokers between competing influences." Caseworkers will be affected by peer-group attitudes, professional values, supervisors' attitudes, management, and community values. Many changes and reforms have already been written into federal welfare regulations, such as provision for advisory boards and the use of paraprofessionals and bilingual aides, which were not previously incorporated into the bureaucracy.[55] With pressure from organized welfare-client groups, such improvements might become a reality, and welfare agencies could be made more responsive to client needs. Public-service agencies must have more empathy with those they are designed to serve. They must not attempt to impose their own moral values upon their clients, nor design their procedures to meet agency desires rather than client needs.

IN CONCLUSION

As Justice Felix Frankfurter indicated years ago in *Joint Anti-Fascist Refugee Committee* v. *McGrath,* due process of law must provide accuracy and legitimacy in judicial or administrative decision making. Weighing the interests of the government and the individual may simply not meet the conditions of these two criteria. Indeed, "rights should protect the individual from the group even — perhaps especially — in cases where injuring the individual would benefit the group."[56] Neither economy nor administrative efficiency can justify denial of due process to any one.[57] Under the dictates of due process, administrative agencies must be concerned that the facts upon which a decision is made to deprive an individual person of government benefits are based on correct information, so that the denied citizen, while never agreeing with the deprivation, will accept the justice of the procedures used. If the procedures followed by an agency served to prejudice substantial interests of the party seeking review, that party should have other avenues of recourse.

When due process protections are not considered an absolute right —

even though they may assume different meanings in different contexts — the lone claimant will face a self-contradictory bureaucracy with little hope of success. The welfare bureaucracy is torn by constitutional and fiscal considerations, as well as requirements to treat the individual fairly, while standardizing the procedures used in dealing with all clients. Due process must be offered the individual claimant in order to shelter him or her from an overloaded bureaucratic routinization.

The present volume has been aimed at exploring comprehensively the management of welfare administration within the context of United States Supreme Court decisions since the appointment of Chief Justice Warren Burger in 1969. The theoretical base under which welfare benefits are offered to the American citizenry has been explored as to whether the receipt of such benefits is a "right" or a "privilege." In other words, is there an entitlement to welfare benefits? The Burger Court decisions through which procedural standards have been established for the administrative consideration of deprivation of benefits have been reviewed and so have the legal issues inherent in these decisions. Lastly, the management problems lying within the administration of welfare have been assessed, principally in terms of the required independence for administrative hearing officers, the possible creation of a separate decision-making body to develop the case law of the administrative sector, and the necessity to meet constitutional due process requirements as well as accurately and efficiently resolving disputes.

While the setting of an AFDC or disability hearing may be casual and, indeed, "friendly," nevertheless the hearing itself has occurred because someone has been denied a benefit to which that person believes he or she is eligible. This creates an adversarial situation. While "adversarial" does not necessarily imply more formalism in procedure, it does indicate a need for all interests to have accurate representation so that the verdict reached will be based on correct and complete information. To expect the lone ALJ — or hearing examiner — to bear the responsibility of seeing that both the claimant's and the government's arguments are adequately presented as well as to decide the merits of the case according to the "substantial evidence" submitted is unreasonable, even in the eyes of the parties themselves. Therefore, legal representatives (perhaps paraprofessionals) should voice the arguments on both sides of the case. This need not abolish the informal atmosphere if the decision maker does not wish, but it ensures a more comprehensive view of the facts of each case. It also enhances the claimant's "right to be heard."

Prehearing conferences might well be useful for the discovery of evidence that might then be stipulated, allowing for a more efficient handling of the hearing. Such stipulations need not, however, exclude the acceptance of a wide range of evidence, including hearsay, which is appropriate to the administrative hearing. The use of official notice also befits the administrative hearing by taking advantage of the expertise acquired by administrative decision makers through years of dealing with the same subject matter. Official notice does not violate due process of law as long as opportunity for rebuttal is afforded.

As well as making administrative hearings more realistic in meeting client needs, the conditions placed upon caseworkers' visiting welfare recipients' homes should also be assessed. A caseworker should not be expected to play the dual role of concern, ostensibly trying to help the recipient escape his or her dependent status and at the same time investigating the recipient's eligibility for benefits. The government needs to become more responsive to the actual needs of welfare clients. Through quality-case management, client needs can be satisfied within the framework of due process of law.

Unfortunately, with the Reagan administration's emphasis upon fiscal conservatism, the economic costs of accuracy and legitimacy will undoubtedly be considered simply too high. The new Chief Executive has made it very clear that he considers that the balance between individual rights and his interpretation of fiscal soundness has swung too long toward the side of the individual. While the new administration has a sincere belief in the ability of a revitalized private sector to provide employment for all, there do not seem to be any answers in terms of how the public sector will be able to guarantee constitutional rights with the drastic budget cuts President Reagan has proposed. Not only will the amount of benefits be reduced − and in some cases, eliminated − but the costs of administrative fairness will not be met.

In his budget message before Congress on February 18, 1981, President Reagan stated that his number one priority was the balancing of the federal budget by 1984. This can be accomplished, he believes, by cutting federal spending $41.4 billion (in March this figure was increased to $48.6 billion), reducing personal income taxes 10 percent during the next three years, accelerating depreciation allowances for business, and reducing federal regulations in the private sector. These reductions will, however, not affect the "social safety net" of basic Social Security retirement benefits, Medicare, and veterans' benefits, so that programs for "the truly deserving needy" will be left untouched. The only portion of the federal budget pie that is to have an increased allocation in fiscal 1982 will be military spending, which is to go up $169.5 billion in 1986 under the Reagan proposal.

While the reductions advocated by the Reagan administration will not adversely affect programs upon which the white middle class rely, they will have a disparate effect upon poor minorities. Cuts in Medicaid, publicly assisted housing, food stamps, public-service jobs, unemployment insurance, and college aid will especially hurt the minorities. Welfare leaders and organized labor have opposed these reductions, as well as the AFDC "workfare" program, which spokesmen see as undercutting normal wage scales by placing AFDC mothers in minimum-wage jobs. Criticism has also been voiced that the administrative costs of the workfare program will not be offset by the productivity rates of the welfare recipients.

A less overt but undoubtedly effective way of penalizing the poor is the Reagan proposal to consolidate over forty federal social programs into four large block grants. States thereby will be given more discretion as to how to spend funds among such programs as energy assistance, child welfare, rehabilitation of the mentally and physically handicapped, community health services, family planning, drug rehabilitation, and black-lung disease. As past experience has demonstrated, some states will spend little or nothing on some programs because of built-in prejudices against potential recipients' rights to such benefits.

Thus far, the SOS Coalition, composed of 115 national organizations of the elderly and disabled, and the Budget Coalition, composed of such groups as the United Auto Workers, the National Education Association, the League of Women Voters, and the National Association for Advancement of Colored People have joined forces to oppose President Reagan's proposals. These groups have aimed their attention at Congress, hoping at least to ameliorate significantly the Reagan program cuts. Congress's reception of these efforts has been mixed, largely because President Reagan has created a skilled and experienced congressional liaison team under the direction of Max L. Friedersdorf, who previously held that position under Gerald Ford. The effectiveness of this team, as well as the warmness of a GOP-controlled Senate, has provided an empathetic sounding board for the Reagan proposals. Even in his February 18 budget message, President Reagan advised Congress that "the people are watching and waiting" for their response to his proposals, so that many Democrats feared being labeled as obstructionists if they opposed the cuts. While the Democratic National Party has been trying to regroup, most Democrats believe that President Reagan will get most of what he asked for.

Congress has used the so-called reconciliation process in an effort to speed along committee consideration of the Reagan package. This means that legislative committees, under the direction of their budget committees, must come up with specific dollar savings in programs under their jurisdiction by a specified date. These savings are then to be voted upon as a whole by Congress, which expedites the matter considerably. To date, the Senate Budget Committee, chaired by Pete V. Domenici (R., New Mexico), recommended $2.3 billion *more* in budget cuts than President Reagan proposed; the Democrats on the committee supported the recommendation. Are these Democrats afraid not to back President Reagan, or are they backing him in order to expedite his failure? Interestingly, the Senate Budget Committee did not support a cut in the cost-of-living increases in the Social Security retirement program which the Reagan administration also sees as too politically volatile among those economic interests that have some political clout.

The Senate Finance Committee and a House Ways and Means subcommittee have also indicated in preliminary votes that they will support the proposed Reagan cuts in Social Security minimum payments, unemployment insurance, welfare, social services, and Medicaid. House Democrats have offered no opposition, and Senate Democratic attempts to moderate the reductions fell on deaf ears. The Senate Finance Committee is chaired by Robert Dole (R., Kansas). On April 2, 1981, the Senate voted 88 to 10 in favor of the Reagan budget.

The Democratic Speaker of the House, Thomas P., "Tip", O'Neill, Jr., has indicated his concern that the Reagan cuts will have much farther-reaching effects than most Americans realize. When the first Reagan budget cut won full congressional support − namely, to repeal a dairy price-support increase scheduled for April 1 − Tip O'Neill was reported by the *Washington Post* to have said that the vote was "a Republican loyalty test and a consumers' vote for Democrats in the big cities." It appears that the American pluralistic political system is not creating *enough* divergent views of the Reagan administration's priorities. if this continues, the greatest losers once again will be the economically disadvantaged in our competitive system − those least able to demand equity.

NOTES AND SOURCES

1: SOURCES OF PUBLIC ASSISTANCE

1. In the context of this study, the following sections of the Social Security Act are significant: 42 U.S.C.
    (a) Old-Age Assistance (grants to states), § § 301–306
    (b) Federal Old-Age, Survivors and Disability Insurance, § § 401–431
    (c) Unemployment Compensation, § § 501–504
    (d) Aid to Needy Families with Children, § § 601–610, § § 620–626, § § 630–644
    (e) Maternal and Child Health and Crippled Children's Services, § § 701–716
    (f) Grants to States for Services to Aged, Blind or Disabled, § § 801–805
    (g) Grants to States for Aid to Blind, § § 1201–1206
    (h) Grants to States for Aid to Permanently and Totally Disabled, § § 1351–1355
    (i) Supplemental Security Incomes for Aged, Blind and Disabled, § § 1381–1385
    (j) Health Insurance for Aged and Disabled, § § 1395–1395pp
    (k) Grants to States for Medical Assistance, § § 1396–1396i
2. Marc Bendick, Jr., Able Lavine, and Toby H. Campbell, *The Anatomy of AFDC Errors* (Washington, D.C.: Urban Institute, 1978), p. 55.
3. Marc Bendick, Jr., and D. Lee Bawden, *Income-Conditioned Programs and Their Clients: A Research Agenda* (Washington, D.C.: Urban Institute, 1977), p. 35.
4. Daniel J. Baum, *The Welfare Family and Mass Administrative Justice* (New York: Praeger Publishers, 1974), pp. 47, 48.
5. John Denvir, "Controlling Welfare Bureaucracy: A Dynamic Approach," *Notre Dame Lawyer* 50 (1975): 474.
6. Charles A. Reich, "Social Welfare in the Public-Private State," *University of Pennsylvania Law Review* 114 (1966): 491, as cited in J. Shelby Wright, "Poverty, Minorities, and Respect for Law," *Duke Law Journal* (1970): 438.
7. Joseph P. Harris, *Congressional Control of Administration* (Washington, D.C.: Brookings Institution, 1964), p. 46.
8. Aaron Wildavsky, *The Politics of the Budgetary Process* (Boston: Little, Brown and Co., 1964), p. 20.

9.   For instance, if a state wishes to enter a matching-funds agreement with the federal government in offering AFDC benefits, it must submit a plan which conforms to the Social Security Act's requirements as well as HEW regulations. 42 U.S.C. § § 601–04, as cited in Baum, p. 11.

10.   42 U.S.C., § § 1395–1396(g) (1970).

11.   42 U.S.C., § § 1381–1383(c) (Supp. II 1972).

12.   42 U.S.C., § § 2701–2994 (1970).

13.   See John C. Donovan, *The Politics of Poverty,* 2d ed. (Indianapolis: Bobbs-Merrill Co., 1973), p. 43.

14.   P.L. No. 94-559, § 2, 90 Stat. 2641 (1976) (amending 42 U.S.C., § 1988 [1970]), enacted October 19, 1976.

15.   45 C.F.R., § 205.10(a)(1) (1973).

16.   Francis Fox Piven and Richard A. Cloward, *Regulating the Poor: The Functions of Public Welfare* (New York: Random House, 1971), p. 130.

17.   Congressional Quarterly, Inc., *The Supreme Court: Justice and the Law,* 2d ed. (Washington, D.C., 1977), p. 32.

18.   Stephen L. Wasby, *Continuity and Change: From the Warren Court to the Burger Court* (Pacific Palisades, Calif.: Goodyear Publishing Company, 1976), p. 24.

19.   James F. Simon, *In His Own Image: The Supreme Court in Richard Nixon's America* (New York: David McKay Co., 1973), p. 74.

20.   Ibid., p. 253.

21.   Wasby, op cit., p. 212.

22.   In the term ending in June 1978, all the Nixon appointees voted together only 36 percent of the time. See Warren Weaver, Jr., "Nixon Appointees to High Court Voting Less as a Bloc with Burger," *New York Times,* 5 July 1978, p. A1.

2: AN ENTITLEMENT TO WELFARE?

1.   Charles A. Reich, "The New Property," *Yale Law Journal* 73 (1964): 733.

2.   See William C. Canby, Jr., "The Burger Court and the Validity of Classifications in Social Legislation: Currents of Federalism," *Arizona State Law Journal* (1975): 5–7.

3.   Reich, op. cit., p. 786.

4.   Charles A. Reich, "Individual Rights and Social Welfare: The Emerging Legal Issues," *Yale Law Journal* 74 (1965): 1245, at 1256.

5.   Robert J. Reinstein, "The Welfare Cases: Fundamental Rights, the Poor, and the Burden of Proof in Constitutional Litigation," *Temple Law Quarterly* 44 (1970): 46.

6.   As to why Justice Marshall, in particular, did not dissent in this decision, must be, and hopefully is, a topic he is saving for his memoirs.

7.   Mark Tuchnet, "The New Property: Suggestion for the Revival of Substantive Due Process," in *The Supreme Court Review,* ed. Philip B. Kurland (Chicago: University of Chicago Press, 1975)., pp. 261–88.

8.   John Rawls, *A Theory of Justice* (Cambridge, Mass.: Harvard University Press, 1971).

9.   Robert Nozick, *Anarchy, State and Utopia* (New York: Basic Books, 1974).

10.   Frank I. Michelman, "In Pursuit of Constitutional Welfare Rights: One View of Rawls' Theory of Justice," *University of Pennsylvania Law Review* 121 (1973): 962.

11.   Ibid., p. 989.

12.   Ibid., p. 1001.

13.   Ibid., p. 1015.

14.   Alan W. Houseman, "Equal Protection and the Poor," *Rutgers Law Review* 30 (1977): 887.

15.   Kenneth M. Davidson, "Welfare Cases and the 'New Majority': Constitutional Theory and Practice," *Harvard Civil Rights-Civil Liberties Law Review* 10 (1975): 513.

16.   Samuel Krislov, "The OEO Lawyers Fail to Constitutionalize a Right to Welfare: A Study in the Uses and Limits of the Judicial Process," *Minnesota Law Review* 58 (1973): 211.

17.   Henry J. Abraham, "'Human' Rights vs. 'Property' Rights: A Comment on the 'Double Standard,'" *Political Science Quarterly* 90 (Summer 1975): 288–92.

18.   William W. Van Alstyne, "The Demise of the Right-Privilege Distinction in Constitutional Law," *Harvard Law Review* 81 (1968): 1444.

3: PROCEDURAL DUE PROCESS IN THE BURGER COURT

1.   Daniel J. Baum, *The Welfare Family and Mass Administrative Justice* (New York: Praeger Publishers, 1974), p. 2.

2.   Congressional Research Service of the Library of Congress, *Administration of the AFDC Program* (Washington, D.C.: U.S. Government Printing Office, 1977) as cited in Toby H. Campbell and Marc Bendick, Jr., *A Public Assistance Data Book (An Urban Institute Paper on Income Security)* (Washington, D.C.: Urban Institute, 1977), pp. 327, 328.

3.   U.S. Department of Health, Education and Welfare, *Handbook of Public Assistance Administration*, pt. 4, sec. 2300(d)(5) (1967).

4.   34 Fed. Reg. 1144 (1969). See *Handbook*, pt. 4, secs. 6200–500.

5.   The Court reinforced an indigent's right to be heard in the courts in Boddie v. Conn., 401 U.S. 371 (1971) (divorce suit) but would not do so for a bankruptcy suit in U.S. v. Kras, 409 U.S. 434 (1973) or for appeal of a welfare denial in Ortwein v. Schwab, 410 U.S. 656 (1973)–all cases involving court filing fees.

6.   See Greene v. McElroy, 360 U.S. 474, 496–97 (1959).

7.   After *Goldberg*, the 1970 HEW regulation requiring the agency to supply counsel to claimants in hearings was repealed because of a shift in agency priorities. Thereafter, the agency was only responsible for informing the claimant of available sources for legal representation.

8.   For a discussion of some of these points, see Michael A. Albert, "Case Comment: 'Due Process of Law—Welfare Recipients' Right to Pretermination Hearing,'" *West Virginia Law Review* 73 (1970–71): 80.

9.   A case involving termination of old-age assistance by the state of California prior to a hearing.

10.   On May 25, 1970, the Court remanded Daniel v. Goliday et al., 398 U.S. 73, to the U.S. District Court for the Northern District of Illinois to apply *Goldberg* to a "reduction" of benefits with the stipulation that the precedent would apply only to termination and suspension of *existing* benefits" (p. 73). Burger, Black, and Stewart dissent.

11.   See Boddie v. Connecticut, 401 U.S., at 378 (1971).

12.   Consolidated Edison Co. v. NLRB, 305 U.S. 197, at 229 (1938).

13.   § 205 (a) and (b) Social Security Act [42 U.S.C. § 405 (a) and (b)]; § 566 (d) APA [5 U.S.C.A. § 556(d)].

14.   42 U.S.C. § 423(d)(1)(A).

15.   42 U.S.C. § 414(a), 415, 423(c)(I) (1970).

16.   Torres v. New York State Department of Labor, 321 F. Supp. 432 (S.D.N.Y.), vacated and remanded; 402 U.S. 968, judgment reinstated, 333 F. Supp. 341 (S.D.N.Y. 1971), aff'd. per curiam, 405 U.S. 949 (1972) petition for rehearing denied, 410 U.S. 971 (1973).

17. See Albert H. Meyerhoff and Jeffrey A. Mishkin, "Application of *Goldberg v. Kelly* Hearing Requirements to Termination of Social Security Benefits," *Stanford Law Review* 26 (1974): 549.
18. 405 U.S., at 221. James B. Cardwell, SSA Commissioner, noted that in 1975, there was a fifty percent reversal rate on disability claims with the Courts approving eighty-four percent of the decisions when challenged. From his testimony before the Subcommittee on Social Security of the Committee on Ways and Means, House of Representatives (Washington, D.C.: Government Printing Office, 1975), pp. 43, 44.
19. Congressional Research Service of the Library of Congress, *Administration of the AFDC Program,* A Report to the Committee on Government Operations, House of Representatives, April 1977, as cited in Toby H. Campbell and Marc Bendick, Jr., *A Public Assistance Data Book* (An Urban Institute Paper on Income Security) (Washington, D.C.: Urban Institute, 1977).
20. See King v. Smith, 392 U.S. 309 (1968) in which the U.S. Supreme Court held invalid an Alabama welfare regulation which disqualified otherwise eligible children from AFDC benefits if their mother cohabited with a man not legally obliged to support them.
21. See (Recent Cases) "Constitutional Law–Search and Seizure–AFDC Caseworker's Visit to Home of Nonconsenting Welfare Recipient not Prohibited by Fourth Amendment," *Vanderbilt Law Review* 24 (1971): 821.
22. See George R. Hodges, "Constitutional Law–*Wyman* v. *James:* The Fourth Amendment in the Balance," *North Dakota Law Review* 50 (1972): 688.
23. 82 Stat. 1213, 18 U.S.C. § 921 et seq.
24. See Barbara Brudno, "Fairness and Bureaucracy: The Demise of Procedural Due Process for Welfare Claimants," *Hastings Law Journal* 25 (1974): 813.
25. Charles A. Reich, "Midnight Welfare Searches and the Social Security Act," *Yale Law Journal* 72 (1963): 1347.
26. See (Note) "Rehabilitation, Investigation and the Welfare Home Visit," *Yale Law Journal* 79 (1970): 746.
27. See Reich, "Individual Rights and Social Welfare," p. 1255.
28. "Rehabilitation, Investigation and the Welfare Home Visit," p. 749.
29. Ibid., pp. 758–60.
30. See also Douglas Q. Wickham, "Restricting Home Visits: Toward Making the Life of the Public Assistance Recipient Less Public," *University of Pennsylvania Law Review* 118 (1970): 1188, who also agrees in making a distinction between welfare investigation and rehabilitation. See King v. Smith, 392 U.S. 309 (1968).
31. (Note) "Administrative Search Warrants," *Minnesota Law Review* 58 (1974): 640.

4: LEGAL ISSUES OF ADMINISTERING PUBLIC ASSISTANCE

1. Paul R. Verkuil, "The Emerging Concept of Administrative Procedure," *Columbia Law Review* 78 (1978): 294.
2. Lewis C. Mainzer, *Political Bureaucracy* (Glenview, Ill.: Scott, Foresman and Co., 1973), p. 33.
3. Ibid., p. 37.
4. Verkuil, p. 279.
5. Senate Bill 2490, "The Regulatory Procedures Reform Act," 95th Congress, 2d Session (1978), superseded by S.262, S.755, and S.2931 (96th Congress).
6. Verkuil, pp. 321–322.
7. Jerry L. Mashaw, et al., *Social Security Hearings and Appeals* (Lexington, Mass.: D.C. Heath and Co., 1978), p. 1.
8. Albert H. Meyerhoff and Jeffrey A. Mishkin, "Application of *Goldberg v. Kelly* Hearing Requirements to Termination of Social Security Benefits," *Stanford Law Review* 26 (1974): 567.

9. Disability Insurance State Manual, DISM § § 265, ID, 353.6A, as cited in Meyerhoff and Mishkin, p. 556, n. 51.

10. John A. Dooley III, and Joseph Goldberg, "The Search for Due Process in the Administration of Social Welfare Programs," *North Dakota Law Review* 47 (1971): 221.

11. First approved by the ABA and the National Conference of Commissioners on Uniform State Laws in 1946, but significantly revised in 1961. Uniform Laws Annotated, Vol. 9c, 1967 Cum. Supp., pp. 134–61. By the end of 1973, accepted as a model by fifty-one states and the District of Columbia.

12. See Stephen A. Subrin and A. Richard Dykstra, "Notice and the Right to Be Heard: The Significance of Old Friends," *Harvard Civil Rights-Civil Liberties Law Review* 9 (1974): 449.

13. In *Goldberg,* the Court specified that notice should probably take the form of a letter and a personal conference with the caseworker to assure that claimants who have difficulty understanding written English *do* receive notice. 397 U.S., at 268.

14. Administrative Procedure in Government Agencies: Report of the Committee on Administrative Procedure (Senate Document No. 8, 77th Congress, 1st Session, 1941) (Charlottesville: University Press of Virginia, 1968), pp. 70, 71.

15. 5 U.S.C.A., § 556(c), (d); § 557(b). But in Mathews v. Eldridge, the Court ruled that the claimant has the burden of continually demonstrating his eligibility for disability benefits, 424 U.S., at 337.

16. *Report of the Disability Claims Process Task Force,* U.S. House of Representatives Subcommittee on Social Security of the Committee on Ways and Means, Gerald L. Boyd, chairman (Washington, D.C.: Government Printing Office, 1975), p. 102.

17. See Daniel Jay Baum, *The Welfare Family and Mass Administrative Justice* (New York: Praeger Publishers, 1974), p. 20, and Appendix A, pp. 74–81.

18. *Administrative Procedure in Government Agencies,* p. 69.

19. See Walter Gellhorn, *Federal Administrative Proceedings,* 2d reprinting (Westport, Conn.: Greenwood Press, 1972), pp. 102–5.

20. Walter Gellhorn and Clark Byse, *Administrative Law: Cases and Comments,* 6th ed. (Mineola, N.Y.: Foundation Press, 1974), pp. 860–2. In Richardson v. Perales, the Court saw written reports by physicians as appropriate within the framework of Professor Gellhorn's five factors. 402 U.S., at 402.

21. Gellhorn, *Federal Administrative Proceedings,* p. 113.

22. Ernest Gellhorn, *Administrative Law and Process* (St. Paul: West Publishing Co., 1972), pp. 208, 209.

23. *Report of the Disability Claims Process Task Force,* p. 101.

24. Robert S. Lorch, *Democratic Process and Administrative Law* (Detroit: Wayne State University Press, 1969), p. 132.

25. One source notes thirty-two exceptions to the hearsay rule plus exceptions on exceptions. Talbot Smith, "The Hearsay Rule and the Docket Crisis," *American Bar Association Journal* 54 (1968): 922–4, as cited in Ernest Gellhorn, *Administrative Law,* p. 222.

26. Ernest Gellhorn, *Administrative Law and Process,* p. 191.

27. NLRB v. Remington Rand, 94 F. 2d 862, 873 (2d Cir.) (Judge Learned Hand). This quotation is paraphrased in the Model State APA, Sec. 10(1).

28. Ernest Gellhorn, *Administrative Law and Process,* pp. 184–8.

29. See Baum, Appendix A, pp. 74–81.

30. 36 Fed. Reg. 3034 (1971); 45 C.F.R. § 205.10(a)(6) (1972). See Carol Clemons et al., "Developments in Welfare Law," *Cornell Law Review* 59 (1974): 927.

31. William D. Popkin, "The Effect of Representation in Nonadversary Proceedings–A Study of Three Disability Programs," *Cornell Law Review* 62 (1977): 989.

32. Gellhorn and Byse, p. 860.

33. Ernest Gellhorn, *Administrative Law and Process*, p. 206.
34. See Baum, Appendix A, pp. 74–81.
35. Lecture by Judge Arthur A. Gladstone, "Trial Techniques: A View from the Bench," given at the National Judicial College, Reno, Nevada, 23 April 1979. See also Frederick Davis, "Judicialization of Administrative Law: The Trial-Type Hearing and the Changing Status of the Hearing Officer," *Duke Law Journal* (1977): 391.
36. 37 Fed. Reg. 16, 787 (1972).
37. Wayne McCormack, "The Purpose of Due Process: Fair Hearing or Vehicle for Judicial Review," *Texas Law Review* 52 (1974): 1259.
38. Gellhorn and Byse, p. 962.
39. Frederick Davis, "Judicialization of Administrative Law: The Trial-Type Hearing and the Changing Status of the Hearing Officer," *Duke Law Journal* (1977): 401.
40. Walter Gellhorn, *Federal Administrative Proceedings*, pp. 26–35.
41. Gellhorn and Byse, pp. 1118–20.
42. Baum, Appendix A, pp. 74–81.
43. *Disability Insurance Amendments of 1979*, Report of the Committee on Ways and Means, U.S. House of Representatives, Al Ullman, chairman (Washington, D.C.: Government Printing Office, 1979).
44. In Citizens to Preserve Overton Park, Inc. v. Volpe, 401 U.S. 402 (1971), the Court emphasized the need for the complete hearing record which the Secretary considered. In U.S. v. Florida East Coast Railway, 410 U.S. 224 (1973), the Court ruled on the importance of all findings and conclusions, and their supporting evidence, being placed "on the record."
45. Lecture by Professor Frederick Davis, 23 April 1979.
46. Ernest Gellhorn, *Administrative Law and Process*, p. 46.
47. Gellhorn and Byse, p. 531.

5: THE ADMINISTRATIVE ORGANIZATION AND MOTIVATION

1. Walter Gellhorn, *Federal Administrative Proceedings*, 2d reprinting (Westport, Conn.: Greenwood Press, 1972), pp. 73, 74.
2. Justice Rehnquist has made the flexibility of due process very clear in Arnett v. Kennedy, 416 U.S. 134 (1974), where the nature of the liberty or property issue will determine the due process standard required.
3. HEW *Handbook of Public Assistance*, pt. 4 § § 6000–6999 (1968). See Robert E. Scott, "The Regulation and Administration of the Welfare Hearing Process —The Need for Administrative Responsibility," *William and Mary Law Review* 11 (1969): 291.
4. 33 Fed. Reg. 17853 (1968).
5. J. L. Mashaw, "Welfare Reform and Local Administration of Aid to Families with Dependent Children in Virginia," *Virginia Law Review* 57 (1971): 818.
6. 38 Fed. Reg. 22,006 (1973).
7. 45 C.F.R. § 206.10(a)(6) (1973). See Carol Clemons et al., "Developments in Welfare Law," *Cornell Law Review* 59 (1974): 929.
8. The previous regulation was 36 Fed. Reg. 3034 (1971) which was simply deleted in 1973.
9. 45 C.F.R. § 205.10(a)(5)(i) (1973).
10. 45 C.F.R. § 205.10(a)(4)(i)(A).
11. 45 C.F.R. § 223.20(a)(12) (1973).
12. Robert E. Scott, "The Reality of Procedural Due Process—A Study of the Implementation of Fair Hearing Requirements by the Welfare Caseworker," *William and Mary Law Review* 13 (1972): 725.
13. The Administrative Conference was formed in 1963 and has been a permanent

conference since 1968. It is composed of representatives from various federal agencies, universities, and the legal profession. It meets four times a year.

14.   S.755, 96th Cong., 1st Sess., § 211 (1979). Besides providing that the Administrative Conference create review boards to appraise the performance of ALJs every seven years, the bill also would establish a performance award pay for ALJs (§ 211). Bills of the same general subject matter introduced in the same session were S.262, "The Reform of Federal Regulation Act," giving the Administrative Conference and Congress more review over agency policy, and S.1291, "The Administrative Practice and Regulatory Control Act," also seeking more review of agencies and public participation in their rule making.

15.   Jerry L. Mashaw et al., *Social Security Hearings and Appeals* (Lexington, Mass.: D.C. Heath and Company, 1978), p. xi. In 1975, about 82 percent of the federal administrative hearings were held in the SSA. See Paul Verkuil, "The Emerging Concept of Administrative Procedure," *Columbia Law Review* 78 (1978): 276, at 312.

16.   See Edwin Yourman, "Report on a Study of Social Security Beneficiary Hearings, Appeals, and Judicial Review," in *Recent Studies Relevant to the Disability Hearings and Appeals Crisis,* Subcommittee on Social Security of the Committee on Ways and Means, U.S. House of Representatives (Washington, D.C.: Government Printing Office, 1975), p. 127. Yourman recommends less pressure from the Federal Personnel Management Office in requiring preappointment regulatory expertise of ALJs.

17.   Frederick Davis, "Judicialization of Administrative Law: The Trial-Type Hearing and the Changing Status of the Hearing Officer," *Duke Law Journal* (1977): 391.

18.   A claimant losing his case before an ALJ of the SSA may appeal to the SSA Appeals Council. The council is the internal agency review step immediately prior to judicial review. However, its function is somewhat undefined in terms of whether the council is to establish precedent or deal solely with individual cases.

19.   Yourman, op. cit., pp. 150, 151, 157.

20.   Mashaw et al., op. cit., pp. 105–107.

21.   Davis, op. cit., p. 394.

22.   Interview with Betty Mandzak, Special Projects and Legislative Specialist, Office of Policy and Procedure, OHA, SSA, Arlington, Virginia, 29 March 1979.

23.   Verkuil, pp. 328–329.

24.   Daniel J. Baum, *The Welfare Family and Mass Administrative Justice* (New York: Praeger Publishers, 1974), p. xiii.

25.   Ibid., taken from a paper presented to the Administrative Conference of the United States by Professor Jerry L. Mashaw, University of Virginia Law School, May 1973.

26.   Mashaw et al., op. cit., p. xxiii.

27.   From an interview with Milton Carrow, director of the Center for Administrative Justice, at the Center, Washington, D.C., 30 March 1979.

28.   Davis, op. cit., pp. 406–407.

29.   Mashaw et al., op. cit., pp. 26–27, 43–48.

30.   Ibid., pp. 146–50.

31.   Bernard Schwartz, "Administrative Law: The Third Century," *Administrative Law Review* 29 (1977): 317.

32.   From an interview with Milton Carrow, 30 March 1979.

33.   Yourman, op. cit., p. 163.

34.   This position was taken by former FCC-ALJ Arthur Gladstone in his lecture, "Setting the Stage," and by Professor Abraham Dash in his lecture, "New Trends in Administrative Law," at the National Judicial College, Reno, Nevada, 23 April 1979.

35.   Mashaw et al., op. cit., pp. 110–15.

36. This position was taken by Mr. Milton Carrow, 30 March 1979.
37. Mashaw et al., op. cit., p. xvi.
38. Quoted in Baum, op. cit., p. 2.
39. Yourman, op. cit., p. 136.
40. See Robert M. O'Neil, "Of Justice Delayed and Justice Denied: The Welfare Prior Hearing Cases," in *The Supreme Court Review*, Philip B. Kurland, ed. (Chicago: University of Chicago Press, 1970), pp. 190–4.
41. See E. A. Tomlinson, "Discovery in Agency Adjudication," *Duke Law Journal* (1971): 89. This article outlines the proposal of the Administrative Conference of the United States in June 1970, which specifies the types of discovery appropriate to adjudicatory proceedings.
42. From remarks entitled "Pretrial Procedures" made by Judge Charles R. Richey, U.S. District Court, Washington, D.C., before the Administrative Law Judges Seminar, Reno, Nevada, 17 September 1973.
43. *Administrative Procedure in Government Agencies*, Report of the Committee on Administrative Procedure (Senate Document No. 8, 77th Congress, 1st Session, 1941) (Charlottesville: University Press of Virginia, 1968), pp. 64–66.
44. See Walter Gellhorn, *Federal Administrative Proceedings*, pp. 114, 115.
45. See Verkuil, op. cit., p. 312. These sentiments were also expressed by Professor Frederick Davis in his lecture "New Trends in State Administrative Law," 23 April 1979, and by Attorney John T. Miller, Jr., in his lecture "The Administrative Process: An Attorney's Perspective," 24 April 1979, at the National Judicial College, Reno, Nevada.
46. Mashaw et al., op. cit., pp. 94–98.
47. Ibid., pp. 49, 50.
48. David R. Packard, "Fair Procedure in Welfare Hearings," *Southern California Law Review* 42 (1969): 620.
49. See Leonard S. Rubenstein, "Procedural Due Process and the Limits of the Adversary System," *Harvard Civil Rights–Civil Liberties Law Review* 11 (1976): 48.
50. Florida Statutes Annotated, chapter 120.50–73, (West Supp. 1977). Davis, op. cit., pp. 399–400.
51. Jerry L. Mashaw, "The Management Side of Due Process, Some Theoretical and Litigation Notes on the Assurance of Accuracy, Fairness, and Timeliness in the Adjudication of Social Welfare Claims," *Cornell Law Review* 59 (1974): 772.
52. Professor Mashaw would probably agree with James B. Cardwell, SSA commissioner, that more responsibility should be placed upon state agencies to conduct face-to-face interviews between the denying state employee and the claimant in order to conciliate many disability claims before they are appealed to the OHA. *Delays on Social Security Appeals*, Subcommittee on Social Security of the Committee on Ways and Means, House of Representatives (Washington, D.C.: Government Printing Office, 1975).
53. See "Rehabilitation, Investigation and the Welfare Home Visit," *Yale Law Review* 79 (1970): 476.
54. It has even been suggested that clients should be able to choose their own caseworkers. John Denvir, "Controlling Welfare Bureaucracy: A Dynamic Approach," *Notre Dame Lawyer* 50 (1975): 476. But caseworkers may not have a perception of their own role as being supportive of claimant rights.
55. Denvir, op. cit., pp. 465–469, 472.
56. (Note) "Specifying the Procedures Required by Due Process: Toward Limits on the Use of Interest Balancing," *Harvard Law Review* 88 (1975): 1527.
57. Other authors argue the reasonability of balancing interests, such as Michael Charles Eberhardt, "Constitutional Law—Due Process and Compliance with Processing Requirements for Welfare Applications," *North Carolina Law Review* 50 (1972): 673.

SELECTED SUPPLEMENTAL READINGS

Barrett, St. John. "The New Role of the Courts in Developing Public Welfare Law." *Duke Law Journal* (Fall 1970): 1–23.

Bennett, Robert W. "Liberty, Equality, and Welfare Reform." *Northwestern University Law Review* 68 (March–April 1973): 74–108.

"Constitutional Law–Fourth-Amendment–New York¯State Mandated Home Visit Is Not an Unreasonable Search–Public Assistance Recipients Must Submit–*Wyman v. James.*" *Albany Law Review* 35 (1971): 809–18.

"Constitutional Law–Home Visits as Structured by New York City Department of Social Services Held Not Violative of Fourth Amendment." *Fordham Law Review* 40 (October 1971): 150–9.

"The Constitutional Minimum for the Termination of Welfare Benefits: The Need for and Requirements of a Prior Hearing." *Michigan Law Review* 68 (November 1969): 112–40.

Coven, Mark S., and Fersh, Robert J. "Equal Protection, Social Welfare Litigation and the Burger Court." *Notre Dame Lawyer* 51 (July 1976): 873–97.

Dolzer, Rudolf. "Welfare Benefits as Property Interests: A Constitutional Right to a Hearing and Judicial Review." *Administrative Law Review* 29 (Fall 1977): 525–75.

Friedlander, Walter A., and Apte, Robert Z. *Introduction to Social Welfare.* 4th ed. Englewood Cliffs, N.J.: Prentice-Hall, 1974.

Funston, Richard. "The Double Standard of Constitutional Protection in the Era of the Welfare State." *Political Science Quarterly* 90 (Summer 1975): 261–87.

Gellhorn, Ernest, and Robinson, Glen O. "Perspectives on Administrative Law." *Columbia Law Review* 75 (May 1975): 771–99.

Grey, Thomas C. "Property and Need: The Welfare State and Theories of Distributive Justice." *Stanford Law Review* 28 (May 1976): 877–902.

Malmberg, John A. "1976 Developments in Welfare Law–Aid to Families with Dependent Children." *Cornell Law Review* 62 (August 1977): 1050–92.

Martin, Peter W. "Welfare Law: The Problem of Terminology." *Cornell Law Review* 60 (June 1975): 792–9.

"Miranda Warnings in Welfare Investigations." *Washington University Law Quarterly* (Spring 1973): 455–61.

Montgomery, Richard A. "Right to Assigned Counsel at Welfare 'Fair Hearings.'" *Albany Law Review* 40 (1976): 676–91.

Myers, Joseph Kirk. *"Wyman v. James:* The Epitome of a Judicial 'Red Herring.'" *North Carolina Central Law Journal* 7 (Spring 1976): 404-13.

Nathanson, Nathaniel L. "Probing the Mind of the Administrator: Hearing Variations and Standards of Judicial Review under the Administrative Procedure Act and Other Federal Statutes." *Columbia Law Review* 75 (May 1975): 721-70.

Pearlman, Lise A. "Welfare Administration and the Rights of Welfare Recipients." *Hastings Law Journal* 29 (September 1977): 19-71.

Redwine, Thomas A. "Welfare–Fourth Amendment Rights Re: Worker Visits." *Baylor Law Review* 23 (Summer 1971): 508-13.

Rogan, Richard A. "The Rejected Applicant for General Assistance and His Right to a Review." *Hastings Law Journal* 25 (February 1974): 678-98.

Scheindlin, Shira A. "Legal Services–Past and Present." *Cornell Law Review* 59 (June 1974): 960-88.

Shapek, Raymond A. "Foundations of Legal Attitudes Toward Welfare Recipients' Rights and Privileges: A Survey." *North Carolina Central Law Journal* 4 (Spring 1973): 203-18.

"Withdrawal of Public Welfare: The Right to a Prior Hearing." *Yale Law Journal* 76 (May 1967): 1234-46.

TABLE OF CASES

113

INDEX